CREATIVE PRESSURE COOKING

Beryl Frank

WEATHERVANE
BOOKS

CREDITS

Mirro-Matic Pressure Cookers and Canners
Mirro Aluminum Company
P.O. Box 409
Manitowoc, Wisconsin 54220

Presto
National Presto Industries
Eau Claire, Wisconsin 54701

Thanks to Mr. Gary Christopherson of Presto and Mrs. Gretchen Ziesmer of Mirro, without whose help and encouragement this book would not have come to be—and to the noble family that ate without complaints all the experiments that never found their way into this book.

contents

introduction to pressure cooking

When you discover a new friend, you take time to get to know that friend. Think of your pressure cooker as a brand new friend—a cooking convenience that will save time, enhance family meals, and become a cooking tool to help in your busy life.

an energy saver

The energy supply is dwindling just at a time when our fuel needs are greatest. Efforts must be made to reduce our energy consumption in every way possible—and the kitchen is a good place to start. By using appliances wisely and relying on methods requiring the least amount of fuel, you'll be doing your part toward relieving the urgency of the crisis.

Pressure cooking saves time, money, and energy. It cuts cooking time by two-thirds—saving you up to 300 kitchen hours in a year. Because it uses the lowest level of heat to maintain proper cooking pressure, it cuts down on fuel usage even more.

a bit of history

Homemakers have not always had the option of pressure cooking. Until a French engineer, Denys Papin, invented the "marmite digestor"—the first pressure cooker—in 1679, only more primitive cooking techniques were available. For instance, prehistoric man held a stick over an open fire. He also had to preserve the burning embers, since he could not rekindle the fire if it went out. North American Indians heated food and water by placing them in baskets into which they dropped hot stones. Many years later, when iron was discovered, people hung pots on slanted rods above the flames.

Although Papin's invention was successful in harnessing the power of steam, it was crude and impractical. The first successful home pressure cooker was not developed until 1914. Even that model was complicated—with a top that screwed on and a dial that had to be watched to check pressure.

Today's pressure cooker is sleek and attractive. . . and it operates on an easy-to-understand principle. Water heated to the boiling point (212°F) creates steam. When air is exhausted and steam is not allowed to escape, pressure results, bringing the temperature to *above* boiling (or 250°F at 15 pounds of pressure). Heat is therefore driven into food—so food cooks much faster.

the joys of pressure cooking

Saves time—Foods cook in one-fourth to one-third the time needed by ordinary cooking methods.

Locks in flavor and color—Food cooks in a short period of time with enough liquid to provide steam, and without air.

Keeps flavors separate—Several foods can be cooked together, using a small amount of liquid beneath the rack.

Retains nutrients—Food can be cooked with a small amount of liquid and no air for oxidation, preserving essential vitamins and minerals to a maximum degree.

Watches the budget—Less-expensive cuts of meat cook deliciously tender in less time than is needed by other cooking methods.

Reduces fuel consumption—Foods cook in one-fourth to one-third the time necessary by other methods.

Cuts down on cleanup—Whole meals can be cooked in one pressure cooker.

Adds to kitchen comfort—Heat and cooking odors are minimal.

Makes meals more interesting—Even gourmet dishes can be cooked in a pressure cooker.

the pressure cooker

some do's and don't's of pressure cooking

Before you start to cook with your pressure cooker, familiarize yourself with it. Look over all the parts of your cooker and read the book of instructions that came with it. Then begin to browse through this book.

The instructions given here for the pressure cooker follow the same pattern as your instruction book, although the words are not always exactly the same. For instance, all pressure cookers have a little gadget that controls the pressure. One manufacturer calls it a pressure regulator. Another calls it a pressure control. They are one and the same, and the two terms are used interchangeably in this book.

The pressure control is described by its manufacturer as jiggling when the pressure is reached. The pressure regulator is described as rocking gently. When either of these things occurs, the pressure for cooking has been reached. The recipes in this book usually read—when pressure has been reached, cook for the required number of minutes.

parts of the pressure cooker

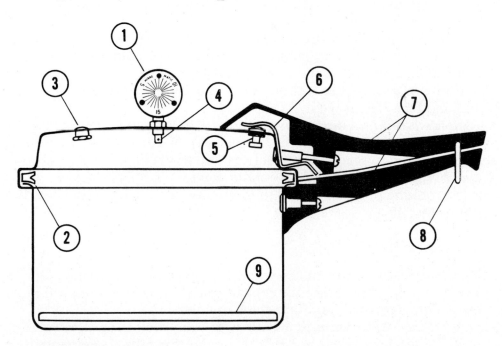

1. automatic pressure control
2. self-sealing gasket
3. safety fuse
4. vent tube
5. lift-pin assembly
6. lock lever
7. comfortable handles
8. reminder ring (not on all models of pressure cookers)
9. all-aluminum cooking rack

Two ways are recommended for immediate cooling of a pressure cooker. One is to put the cooker in a pan of cold water until the air vent has dropped and no steam escapes when the pressure control is tilted. A second and more convenient means of cooling the cooker is to cool the cooker under the water faucet with cold running water. This is the way suggested in the recipes in this book.

When the recipe says to allow the cooker to cool normally, this means remove the pressure cooker from the heat, usually to an unused burner on the stove. The pressure will reduce by itself in about 10 minutes or less. If you move the pressure control and no steam escapes, the pressure has reduced itself and you may remove the cover of the cooker.

timing

One of the nicest things about your pressure cooker is the speed with which you can put a meal together. Like all cooking, a little preplanning saves time in the long run and makes for a smoother dinner on the table.

All the recipes included here have the number of minutes listed for actual cooking time. When a recipe reads "cook for 2 minutes," this means cook for 2 minutes from the time the regulator is gently rocking (in other words, when the proper pressure has been reached).

Remember, it takes the cooker time for the pressure to build up. As a general rule of thumb, allow 5 minutes for the pressure to build—or until the regulator jiggles. If the recipe you use tells you to cool the cooker immediately, you can figure actual time on the flame to be 7 minutes.

When the recipe tells you to allow the cooker to cool naturally, you know you must allow between 10 and 15 minutes for this. When planning your meal, allow time for the cooling period as well as the actual cooking time. You are still saving much time in the actual preparation—and you can judge when to fill the water glasses and toss the salad as well.

Timing is what puts a dinner on the table all at the same time. It is as important to pressure cooking as to any old-fashioned way of cooking. Be sure to allow for both the time needed to reach the pressure as well as the time for natural cooling.

Remember your rule of thumb—about 5 minutes for pressure to build before you time the cooking process, and 10 to 15 minutes extra when you allow the cooker to cool naturally.

clear that vent pipe

All pressure cookers need a clear vent pipe to perform properly. One manufacturer suggests you hold the lid of the cooker up to the light before putting it in place for cooking. This is certainly a good habit to get into.

A pipe cleaner will ensure that your vent tube is clear and clean. If you have given the cooker lid the eye test and it fails, get out that pipe cleaner and use it.

Another way to make sure the vent pipe is clear is to hold it under the faucet and watch the water come through. If this is done after using the cooker, you will be ready with a clear vent pipe when you want to cook again.

fifteen pounds of pressure

The recipes in this book have been prepared using 15 pounds of pressure. If you have a pressure cooker that offers three different pressure gauges, use 15 pounds for the recipes included here. Consult the manufacturer's pamphlet included with your cooker for correct times at lower pressure.

why this book?

This cookbook is not intended to replace the book that comes with your pressure cooker. Read that book carefully. The manufacturer knows what will work in his cooker. Familiarize yourself with the cookbook included with your cooker.

When you are completely comfortable with your own pressure cooker and the recipes that came with it, you will be ready to try new things. Hopefully, you will find those new things here—in suggestions from plain to fancy cooking.

cream of asparagus soup

Yield: 4 to 6 servings

1 pound fresh asparagus, cut into
    1-inch pieces
1 slice lemon
2 cups chicken broth
1 tablespoon cornstarch

¼ cup water
1 cup milk and 1 cup
    cream, heated
1 teaspoon salt
¼ teaspoon pepper

Put asparagus, lemon, and chicken broth into cooker. Close cover and put pressure control in place. When pressure is reached, cook for 2 minutes. Cool at once under running water.

Blend cornstarch in water. Add to open cooker, stirring until slightly thickened. Add heated milk and cream, salt, and pepper. Simmer 1 minute.

Serve in soup bowls.

cream of asparagus soup

green-bean soup

Yield: 4 to 6 servings

1 pound green beans, cut into 1-inch pieces	¼ cup cold water
4 cups beef or chicken broth	½ teaspoon sugar
1 tablespoon cornstarch	½ teaspoon salt
	½ cup sour cream

Put beans and broth into cooker. Close cover and set pressure control in place. When pressure is reached, cook for 3 minutes. Cool cooker at once under running water. Return open cooker to a low flame.

Mix cornstarch and water; add to soup, stirring until thickened slightly. Season with sugar and salt; blend in sour cream.

Serve soup at once.

beet soup

Yield: 4 to 6 servings

2 large beets, diced	1 tablespoon flour
1 tablespoon vinegar	¼ cup water
½ teaspoon salt	1 small beet, grated
2 teaspoons sugar	Sour cream for garnish
4 cups beef broth	

Put beets in cooker. Add vinegar, salt, sugar, and beef broth. Close cover and set pressure regulator in place. When pressure is reached, cook for 10 minutes. Cool at once under running water. Remove cooker cover.

Mix flour and water thoroughly; add to soup. Stir over a low flame until mixture thickens slightly. Sprinkle the grated beet on top of the soup.

Serve in soup bowls. Garnish with a spoonful of sour cream.

cold beet soup

Yield: 4 to 6 servings

1 bunch young red beets with tops, sliced	½ teaspoon sugar
1 tablespoon lemon juice	1 large cucumber, peeled and thinly sliced
½ cup water	2 hard-boiled eggs, sliced
2 cups buttermilk	2 teaspoons dill leaves
½ cup sour cream	1 tablespoon chopped green onion
½ cup liquid from cooked beets	

Place beets, lemon juice, and water in cooker. Close cover and set presure regulator in place. When pressure is reached, cook for 5 minutes. Cool at once under running water. Drain beets; reserve the liquid. Chill.

Mix buttermilk, sour cream, and beet liquid. Add sugar. Put chilled beets, cucumber, eggs, dill, and green onion into buttermilk mixture. Blend.

Serve soup very cold.

corn chowder

To vary the chowder, you might include celery, broccoli, or cauliflower in season.

Yield: 4 to 6 servings

> 3 tablespoons butter or margarine
> 1 large onion, chopped
> 1 10-ounce package frozen corn
> 2 cups canned tomatoes
> 1 large potato, diced
> ½ cup water
> 2 teaspoons salt
> Dash of pepper
> 3 cups milk
> 2 tablespoons cornstarch
> Liberal sprinkling of parsley

Melt butter in cooker; lightly tan the onion. Add vegetables, ¼ cup water, salt, and pepper. Close cooker and put pressure regulator in place. When pressure is reached, cook for 2 minutes. Cool cooker at once. Remove pressure control and top. Return cooker to low flame.

Add milk and bring just to a boil. Mix the cornstarch with ¼ cup water; add to cooker. Stir for 1 minute more to slightly thicken chowder.

Garnish with parsley; serve.

romaine-lettuce soup

Yield: 4 to 6 servings

> 1 small onion, minced
> 2 tablespoons shortening
> 4 cups chopped romaine lettuce
> 1 teaspoon salt
> ¼ teaspoon pepper
> 4 cups chicken broth
> 2 egg yolks
> ½ cup heavy cream

Tan onion in heated shortening. Add lettuce, salt, pepper, and broth. Close cover and put pressure control in place. When pressure is reached, remove from heat and cool cooker under running water. Return open cooker to low flame.

Beat together the egg yolks and heavy cream. Stir into the soup mixture. Do not boil. When soup begins to thicken, add extra salt if desired. Serve.

leek soup

Yield: 4 to 6 servings

> 4 leeks, washed, sliced lengthwise, and cut into 1-inch pieces
> 2 tablespoons butter or margarine
> 2 large onions, chopped
> 4 cups chicken or beef broth
> ½ teaspoon salt
> 1 cup milk
> 1 cup diced ham

Wash leeks and cut into 1-inch pieces.

Melt butter in cooker; sauté the leeks. Add the chopped onions. When leeks are soft, add broth and salt. Close cover of cooker and put pressure control in place. When pressure is reached, cook for 3 minutes. Cool cooker at once.

Return open cooker to a low flame. Add milk and ham; simmer for 3 minutes more. Serve.

fresh-okra soup

Yield: 4 to 6 servings

1 pound fresh okra, chopped fine	1 teaspoon salt
	½ teaspoon pepper
1 medium onion, chopped	1 bay leaf
4 fresh tomatoes, diced	4 cups beef broth

Put all ingredients into cooker in order given. Close cover and put pressure control in place. When pressure is reached, cook for 3 minutes. Cool cooker at once.

Since this is a Southern specialty, serve it with rice and cornbread.

leek soup

onion soup

Yield: 4 to 6 servings

2 tablespoons shortening
2 cups thinly sliced onions
4 cups beef broth

Seasoned croutons
Parmesan cheese

Heat shortening in cooker; lightly tan onions. Add beef broth. Close cover and set pressure control in place. When pressure is reached, cook for 3 minutes. Cool at once under running water.

Serve soup in individual serving bowls, topped with croutons and Parmesan cheese.

potato soup

Yield: 4 to 6 servings

2 cups diced potatoes
2 scallions, chopped
4 cups chicken broth

1 cup milk
1 teaspoon Worcestershire sauce
½ cup sour cream

Combine potatoes, scallions, and broth in cooker. Close cover and put pressure control in place. When pressure is reached, cook for 4 minutes. Cool cooker at once.

Spoon out the solid vegetables; put them through a sieve to mash fine. Return the vegetables to the broth; simmer. Gradually add milk, Worcestershire sauce, and sour cream.

Serve soup either hot or cold.

onion soup

potato and cucumber soup

Yield: 4 to 6 servings

6 medium potatoes, diced
1 medium cucumber,
   diced
1 small onion, grated

1 teaspoon salt
¼ teaspoon pepper
1 teaspoon dillweed
2 cups milk or cream

Put potatoes, cucumber, onion, salt, pepper, and dillweed into cooker. Close cover and set pressure control in place. When pressure is reached, cook for 5 minutes. Cool cooker at once.

Return open cooker to a low flame. Stir in the milk gradually, allowing all to blend and heat.

Serve in tureen or individual soup bowls.

potato and cucumber soup

16

pumpkin soup

Use your Halloween jack-o-lantern for this soup and enjoy every mouthful.

Yield: 4 to 6 servings

2 cups fresh pumpkin, cut into
1-inch pieces
3 cups chicken broth
2 tablespoons brown sugar

½ teaspoon ginger
½ teaspoon cinnamon
½ cup finely chopped ham
1 cup light cream

Put pumpkin and chicken broth into cooker. Close cover and set pressure control in place. When pressure is reached, cook for 5 minutes. Cool at once under running water. Open cooker and return to low heat.

Add the rest of ingredients in order given. Simmer soup until hot; do not boil. Serve soup at once.

rice broth with parsley and celery

Yield: 4 servings

1 cup uncooked rice
1 cup chopped celery
¼ cup minced parsley
1 teaspoon salt
4 cups beef or chicken stock

Place all ingredients in cooker in order listed. Close cover and set pressure regulator in place. When pressure is reached, remove cooker from heat. Allow to cool naturally.

Broth is ready to serve.

rice broth with parsley and celery

sauerkraut soup

Yield: 4 to 6 servings

 1 pound sauerkraut (large can, well-drained)
 1 large onion, diced
 1 tablespoon sugar
 4 cups beef broth
 1 tablespoon cornstarch
 ¼ cup water
 Salt and pepper

Place sauerkraut, onion, sugar, and beef broth in cooker. Close cover securely and set pressure control in place. When pressure control jiggles, cook for 10 minutes. Cool at once under running water.

Mix cornstarch with water; add to soup, stirring constantly until slightly thickened. Season with salt and pepper to taste. Serve.

spinach soup

Yield: 4 servings

 1 pound fresh spinach or 1 package frozen chopped spinach
 1 quart chicken stock
 1 tablespoon cornstarch
 ¼ cup water
 1 teaspoon salt
 Dash of ground pepper
 ¼ teaspoon nutmeg

Wash and chop spinach coarsely. If frozen spinach is used, thaw completely and drain.

Put chicken stock into cooker with chopped spinach. Close cover and set pressure control in place. When pressure is reached, cook for 1 minute. Reduce pressure instantly under running water.

Mix cornstarch with water; add to soup. Stir constantly until slightly thickened. Add salt, pepper, and nutmeg. Simmer for 1 minute more; serve.

hot tomato soup

Yield: 4 to 6 servings

½ cup rice
1 medium onion, quartered
2 cups cut-up fresh tomatoes
2 to 3 hot red peppers
½ teaspoon salt
1 teaspoon sugar
4 cups water
Parsley for garnish

Put ingredients into cooker in order listed (except parsley). Close cover on cooker and put pressure regulator in place. When pressure is reached, cook for 1 minute. Remove cooker from heat and allow to cool naturally.

Serve in soup bowls, garnished with parsley.

hot tomato soup

vegetable soup

This is truly a vegetable soup enhanced by the vitamins and flavor of the vegetables used.

Yield: 4 to 6 servings

1 cup diced carrots
1 cup fresh green peas
1 cup cauliflower florets
½ cup diced potatoes
¼ cup fresh green beans

8 halves small red
   radishes
2 teaspoons salt
4¼ cups water
1 tablespoon cornstarch

Put vegetables into cooker as listed, with salt and 4 cups water. Close cover and set pressure control in place. When pressure is reached, cook for 5 minutes. Cool cooker at once under running water.

Mix cornstarch with ¼ cup water; add to soup. Stir until clear color returns and liquid thickens slightly. Serve.

vegetable soup

dutch vegetable soup

Yield: 4 to 6 servings

2 tablespoons shortening
½ pound beef cubes,
    cut small
¼ cup rice
1 cup diced carrots
A few Brussels sprouts
½ cup diced celery
1 leek
½ cup cauliflower florets
2 teaspoons salt
½ teaspoon pepper
Parsley for garnish

Melt shortening in cooker; brown beef. Add rest of ingredients (except parsley); close cover of cooker. Put pressure control in place. When pressure is reached and control jiggles gently, cook for 15 minutes. Cool cooker at once under running water.

Garnish soup with parsley, and serve.

summer vegetable soup

Yield: 4 to 6 servings

1 cup diced carrots
1 cup fresh green peas
1 cup cauliflower florets
½ cup diced new
    potatoes
2 teaspoons salt
½ teaspoon pepper
3¼ cups water

1 tablespoon cornstarch
1 cup milk
1 egg yolk
¼ cup heavy cream
½ pound shrimp, cooked
    and cleaned
Chopped parsley or dill
    for garnish

Put carrots, peas, cauliflower, potatoes, salt, pepper, and 3 cups water into the cooker. Close cover and put pressure regulator in place. When pressure is reached, cook for 2 minutes. Cool at once under running water. Open cooker and return to a very low flame.

Mix cornstarch in ¼ cup water; add to the vegetable soup. Gradually add the milk.

Combine egg yolk and cream in a small bowl. Add 1 cup of the soup stock. Mix with a whisk. Add the mixture back into the soup, followed by the shrimp. Simmer for 3 minutes more. Add seasonings if necessary, such as more salt and pepper.

Pour into a soup tureen or serve in individual bowls, garnishing each portion with chopped parsley or dill.

vegetable chowder

Yield: 4 to 6 servings

> 1 large onion, chopped
> 3 tablespoons butter or margarine
> 1 package frozen corn (about 1 cup heavy)
> 1 package frozen baby lima beans
> 1 large potato, diced
> 1 cup water
> 2 teaspoons salt
> Dash of pepper
> 3 cups milk
> 2 tablespoons cornstarch
> Liberal sprinkling of parsley

Sauté the onion in butter in cooker. When onion is lightly tanned, add vegetables, ¾ cup water, salt, and pepper. Close cover of cooker and put pressure control in place. When pressure is reached and control jiggles, cook for 2 minutes. Cool cooker at once under running water. Remove pressure control and top. Return to low flame.

Add milk to the vegetables; bring to a boil. Mix the cornstarch with ¼ cup water; add to the chowder. Stir continuously for 1 more minute.

Serve chowder with hot rolls and a salad. This will fill them up.

peasant soup

Peasants have very good taste, you'll agree.

Yield: 4 to 6 servings

> 4 cups diced vegetables (any in season)
> 2 onions, diced
> 1 teaspoon salt
> ½ teaspoon pepper
> 4 cups water
> ½ cup sour cream

Put all vegetables into the cooker. Add salt, pepper, and water. Close cover on cooker. Set pressure regulator in place. When pressure is reached, cook for 5 minutes. Cool at once under running water.

Stir in the sour cream and simmer until hot.

Serve soup at once.

10-minute vichyssoise

This free-and-easy treat for a summer day can be prepared in the cool of the morning in a very short time. Chill through the day and serve as the sun sets.

Yield: 4 to 6 servings

> 2 cups diced potatoes
> 1 medium onion, chopped
> 2 cups chicken broth
> 1 teaspoon salt
> 2 cups milk or cream
> 1 tablespoon chopped chives

Put potatoes, onion, and chicken broth into cooker. Close cover and set pressure regulator in place. When regulator is rocking gently, cook for 5 minutes. Cool at once.

Mash the potatoes and liquid through a sieve into a large bowl. Add salt and milk; mix well to blend all the flavors.

Garnish vichyssoise with chives when ready to serve.

chilled cherry soup

Yield: 4 to 6 servings

> ½ cup raisins
> 6 thin orange slices
> 6 thin lemon slices
> 1 cup sliced fresh peaches
> 2 cups pitted cherries
> ½ cup sugar
> ½ teaspoon cinnamon
> Dash of salt
> 1 cup water
> 1 tablespoon cornstarch
> Whipped cream for garnish

Put fruit, sugar, cinnamon, salt, and water into cooker. Close cover and put pressure control in place. When pressure is reached, remove from heat and cool cooker at once under running water.

Remove ¼ cup liquid from fruit. Mix cornstarch with this; return to open cooker. Stir for 1 minute more as mixture thickens slightly. Put in a bowl and chill.

When served, garnish soup with whipped cream.

Picture on next page: 10-minute vichyssoise

fruit soup

This is a Scandinavian specialty which may be served either hot or cold, for dessert, as a first course, or even for breakfast.

Yield: 4 to 6 servings

¼ pound pitted prunes
1 cup currants
1 cup fresh apples, quartered
1 quart water
½ cup cooked rice
3 tablespoons tapioca
¼ cup sugar
1 cinnamon stick
1 tablespoon lemon juice

Combine prunes, currants, apples, and water in cooker. Close cover and set pressure control in place. When pressure is reached, cook for 5 minutes. Allow cooker to cool normally for 5 minutes, then reduce pressure under running water.

Add cooked rice and tapioca to mixture; cook until clear. Add sugar, cinnamon stick, and lemon juice; cook for 2 minutes more, stirring gently.

Serve soup either hot or cold.

almond soup

Yield: 4 to 6 servings

2 cups water
½ teaspoon salt
1 cup white rice
2 teaspoons lemon juice
2 cups milk
¼ pound grated almonds
¼ cup sugar
1 teaspoon almond extract
¼ cup raisins

Combine water, salt, rice, and lemon juice in cooker. Close cover securely and set pressure control in place. When pressure is reached and control is jiggling gently, remove from heat. Allow to cool normally. Remove the cover.

Add milk, almonds, sugar, almond extract, and raisins to the rice. Stir until all ingredients are hot and blended.

Since this is a sweet soup, it is good served after the meat course.

coconut soup

Yield: 4 to 6 servings

2 ounces shredded
    coconut
4 cups chicken stock
1 teaspoon salt

2 tablespoons cornstarch
¼ cup water
1 cup milk or cream
Pinch of nutmeg

Combine coconut, chicken stock, and salt in cooker. Close cover and put pressure control in place. When pressure is reached, cook for 3 minutes. Cool at once under running water. Return open cooker to a very low flame.

Mix cornstarch and water together; add to the soup. Stir constantly until slightly thickened. Add milk gradually. Simmer, but do not boil.

Serve in soup bowls with a pinch of nutmeg sprinkled on top.

peanut soup

Yield: 4 to 6 servings

1 pound fresh peanuts, blanched
    and grated
1 cup milk
3 cups beef stock

1 teaspoon salt
1 tablespoon cornstarch
¼ cup water
1 cup cream

Put grated peanuts, milk, beef stock, and salt into cooker. Close cover securely and put pressure regulator in place. When pressure is reached and regulator rocks gently, remove from heat. Cool cooker at once under running water. Return open cooker to low flame.

Mix cornstarch and water; add to soup. Stirring constantly, add cream gradually.

Dish into soup bowls. Serve.

beef and cabbage soup

Yield: 4 to 6 servings

2 tablespoons shortening
½ pound ground beef
½ cup shredded cabbage
4 small potatoes, diced
1 carrot, diced

1 parsnip, diced
1 medium onion, chopped coarse
2 teaspoons salt
¼ teaspoon fresh ground pepper
4 cups beef broth

Melt shortening in cooker; brown ground beef thoroughly. Add the rest of the ingredients in order given. Close cover and set pressure regulator in place. When pressure is reached, cook for 15 minutes. Allow pressure to drop of its own accord. Serve.

chicken and broccoli soup

Yield: 4 servings

1 package frozen chopped broccoli
½ cup chicken broth
½ teaspoon salt
¼ teaspoon pepper
1 10-ounce can cream of celery soup
1 cup heavy cream
1 cup diced, cooked chicken
Parsley for garnish (optional)

Allow broccoli to thaw until it can be broken up.

Put broccoli, chicken broth, salt, and pepper into cooker. Close cover and set pressure control in place. When pressure is reached, cook for 2 minutes. Cool at once under running water.

Put cooked broccoli on a low flame. Add cream of celery soup, heavy cream, and chicken. Stir constantly but gently until soup is hot. Do not boil.

Garnish soup with parsley if desired. Serve.

chicken and corn soup

Yield: 4 to 6 servings

2 whole chicken breasts, halved
2 cups fresh corn
1 onion, quartered
2 teaspoons salt
¼ teaspoon saffron
¼ teaspoon pepper
4 cups water
1 teaspoon chopped parsley
2 hard-cooked eggs, chopped

Put chicken, corn, onion, salt, saffron, pepper, and water into cooker. Close cover and set pressure control in place. When pressure is reached, cook for 15 minutes. Cool cooker at once under running water.

Remove chicken breasts and take meat from bones. Dice the cooked meat and return it to the soup. Simmer the soup for 2 to 3 minutes more.

Garnish soup with parsley and chopped eggs. Serve.

turkey soup

There's always a turkey carcass at holiday time. The following soup meal is an economical dinner that uses leftover turkey bones.

Yield: 4 to 6 servings

    5 cups water
    1 large potato, diced (about 2 cups)
    1 large onion, quartered
    ½ cup diced carrots
    ½ cup chopped celery
    2 teaspoons salt
    ¼ teaspoon pepper
    1 leftover turkey carcass

Combine water, vegetables, salt, and pepper in the cooker. Bring this to a boil. *Then*, add turkey bones and close cover of cooker. Put on the pressure regulator. When pressure is reached and regulator is rocking gently, cook for 20 minutes. Allow pressure to drop of its own accord.

Remove the large bones, clean off the meat, and return meat scraps to soup.

Serve in soup bowls.

turkey soup

giblet soup

Once you try this, you'll save all your giblets for soup. Easy, fast and different.

Yield: 4 servings

> 1 cup cubed chicken or
>   turkey giblets
> 1 teaspoon salt
> 1 medium onion, chopped
> 1 stalk celery, diced
> 1 cup rice
> 4 cups chicken broth
> Freshly grated nutmeg

Put all ingredients except nutmeg into cooker. Close cover and put pressure control in place. When pressure is reached and control jiggles, remove from heat and allow cooker to cool of its own accord.

Stir the soup and serve in soup bowls. Don't forget that generous dash of nutmeg. It gives an extra-special flavor.

maryland crab soup

Yield: 4 to 6 servings

> 1 large onion, chopped
> 1 stalk celery, diced
> 2 tablespoons shortening
> 2 cups crab meat, picked to
>   remove shell
> 4 cups chicken broth
> ½ teaspoon salt
> ½ teaspoon pepper
> ½ cup heavy cream
> 2 tablespoons whiskey
>   (optional)
> Parsley for garnish

Cook onion and celery in shortening until transparent. Add crab meat, broth, salt and pepper. Close cover and put pressure control in place. When pressure is reached and control jiggles, remove from heat. Cool cooker at once under running water.

Return open cooker to low flame. Add cream, stirring until hot; do not boil. Last, add whiskey.

Serve soup at once with parsley garnish.

29

fish and bacon chowder

Yield: 4 to 6 servings

2 pounds fish fillets, cut into
  serving pieces
2 cups diced potatoes
1 large onion, quartered
1 teaspoon salt
Dash of pepper

1¼ cups water
1 tablespoon cornstarch
6 strips of cooked bacon
  in bits
1 cup milk or cream
Parsley for garnish

Place fish, potatoes, onion, salt, pepper, and 1 cup water into cooker. Close cover and put pressure regulator in place. When pressure is reached, cook for 4 minutes. Cool cooker at once under running water. Set cooker open on a low flame.

Mix ¼ cup water with cornstarch; add to open cooker. Stir; add the bacon bits as mixture thickens slightly. Last, add the milk; simmer for just 2 minutes more.

Serve in soup bowls, garnished with parsley, if desired.

polish fish broth

Yield: 4 to 6 servings

1½ pounds fish, cut into
  1-inch pieces
2 carrots, diced
2 celery stalks, diced
1 large onion, chopped
1 cup shredded cabbage

5 peppercorns
1 bay leaf
1 teaspoon salt
2 cups water
¼ teaspoon nutmeg

Put all ingredients (except nutmeg) into cooker. Close cover securely and set pressure control in place. When pressure is reached, cook for 3 minutes. Cool cooker at once under running water.

Add nutmeg; simmer for 1 minute more.

Serve broth at once.

polish fish broth

beef pot roast I

Yield: 4 to 6 servings

1 tablespoon shortening
4 pounds beef pot roast
Salt and pepper
1 onion, minced
1 bay leaf
1 cup water

Heat shortening in cooker and brown the roast on all sides. Add the seasonings and water in the order given. Cover the cooker and set pressure control in place. When the control is gently rocking, cook for 35 minutes. Allow the pressure to drop naturally.

Remove the roast and slice for serving. If gravy is wanted, thicken the essence left in the cooker.

beef pot roast II

Yield: About 6 servings

2 tablespoons shortening
1 3- to 4-pound pot roast
4 teaspoons salt
1 large onion chopped or 1 package onion soup mix
1 tablespoon Worcestershire sauce
½ cup chili sauce
¾ cup water

Heat shortening in cooker and brown the pot roast on all sides. Add rest of ingredients in the order given. Close cover and set pressure control in place. When pressure is reached, cook for 35 minutes. Allow pressure to drop naturally.

Thicken gravy if desired. Serve.

beef pot roast I

sweet-and-sour pot roast

This is a delicious dinner that can be prepared 1 hour before you eat it. It is also a company dish in its own right.

Yield: 6 servings

4 pounds beef pot roast, brisket or chuck	2 tablespoons shortening
1 teaspoon nutmeg	2 onions, sliced
1 teaspoon cinnamon	1 clove garlic, diced
½ teaspoon ginger	(optional)
2 teaspoons salt	½ cup sugar
Dash of pepper	½ cup red wine
	½ cup water

Rub the raw meat with a combination of nutmeg, cinnamon, ginger, salt, and pepper.

Place shortening in the cooker and allow to heat. Brown the meat well on all sides. Add the onions and garlic.

Dissolve the sugar in the wine and water and pour into cooker. Close cover securely, put on the pressure regulator and allow pressure to come up. When regulator is gently rocking, cook the meat for 40 minutes. Allow the pressure to drop of its own accord, about 10 minutes.

Slice and serve the roast.

brisket with wine

Yield: 4 to 6 servings

3- to 4-pound brisket
1 tablespoon shortening
Salt and pepper to taste
1 onion, minced
1 cup red wine

Brown the meat on all sides in the shortening. Add seasonings, onion, and red wine. Place cover on cooker and set pressure regulator in place. When the pressure is reached, cook for 35 minutes. Allow the pressure to drop naturally.

Slice and serve the brisket with gravy from the essence if desired.

Another variation of this is to use orange juice in place of the wine.

beef cubes in sherry

Yield: 4 to 6 servings

2 tablespoons shortening
2 pounds lean stewing beef,
    cubed
1 package onion soup mix

1 cup sherry wine
1 can cream of mushroom soup
1 teaspoon garlic salt
¼ pound sliced mushrooms

Heat shortening in cooker. Brown the beef cubes on all sides. Add the remaining ingredients in order given. Close cover of cooker. Put pressure control in place. When pressure is reached, cook for 15 minutes. Allow cooker to cool normally.

Serve beef over broad noodles. Delicious!

pepper steak

Yield: 4 servings

1½ pounds round steak,
    ¾ inch thick
1 tablespoon finely crushed
    whole black peppercorns

1 tablespoon shortening
½ cup water
1 tablespoon cognac
½ cup heavy cream

Trim the fat off steak and coat the steak well with crushed peppercorns, pressing them into the meat. Set aside for 1 hour.

Heat shortening in cooker. Brown the steak on both sides. Add water. Close cover and put pressure control in place. When pressure is reached, cook 15 minutes. Let pressure drop normally.

Remove the steak to a heated platter. Add cognac and heavy cream to the liquid in cooker. Bring to a boil, but do not boil, stirring until hot and well-blended.

Pour sauce over the steak. Serve.

stuffed flank steak

Yield: 4 servings

1 large 1-pound flank steak
Salt and pepper

stuffing

¾ cup sausage meat
1 apple, peeled and sliced
1½ cups dried bread crumbs
1 tablespoon finely minced onion
¼ teaspoon salt
3 tablespoons shortening
¾ cup water

Trim edges of flank steak and sprinkle with salt and pepper. Set aside.

Brown the sausage in a fry pan and pour off excess fat. Add the apple, bread crumbs, onion, and salt. Mix together well. Spread this mixture over the flank steak and roll steak up loosely, tying it securely.

Put shortening in pressure cooker and brown the tied steak on all sides. Add water, cover securely, and set pressure control in place. After control jiggles, cook for 35 minutes. Cool cooker naturally for 5 minutes, then reduce pressure under running water.

If gravy is desired, thicken the essence that is in the cooker and pour over flank steak. Serve.

beef cubes in sherry

34

short ribs hawaiian

Yield: 4 to 6 servings

1 onion, sliced into thin rings	¼ teaspoon pepper
2 tablespoons shortening	1 teaspoon garlic salt
3 pounds beef short ribs	2 tablespoons chopped
1 teaspoon ginger	parsley
2 teaspoons dry mustard	2 tablespoons soy sauce
2 tablespoons sugar	2 tablespoons vinegar
1 teaspoon salt	½ cup water

Gently sauté onion rings in shortening. When onion rings are yellow and soft, remove from cooker.

Brown the ribs on all sides, adding extra shortening if needed.

Mix the remaining ingredients and pour over the ribs. Close cover and put regulator in place. When pressure is reached, cook for 25 minutes. Allow the ribs to cool naturally.

Serve the ribs with rice and a pineapple salad to complete the flavor of the islands.

short ribs in teriyaki sauce

Yield: 4 servings

2 pounds short ribs
Teriyaki sauce to cover the ribs
½ cup water

Marinate the short ribs in teriyaki sauce for at least 1 hour.

Place the ribs and marinade in cooker, adding the water. Close the cover of the cooker and place control on. When pressure is reached, cook for 25 minutes. Allow this to cool naturally. Serve.

cabbage rolls

Yield: 4 servings

Boiling water	1 small onion, chopped fine
8 large cabbage leaves	1 cup cooked rice
1 pound ground beef	1 egg
1 teaspoon salt	1 10½-ounce can tomato soup
¼ teaspoon pepper	¾ cup water

Pour boiling water over the cabbage leaves and let stand for 5 minutes. Drain.

Combine meat, salt, pepper, onion, cooked rice, and egg. This mixture is the filling for the cabbage leaves. Roll some into each leaf, closing the rolls with toothpicks.

Place rack in cooker and put cabbage rolls on the rack. Pour the tomato soup and ¾ cup water over the rolls. Close cover and put pressure control in place. When control rocks gently, cook for 8 minutes. Allow to cool naturally for 5 minutes, then put cooker under faucet to cool the rest of the way. Serve.

Picture on previous page: pepper steak

meat and cabbage balls

Yield: 6 servings

Boiling water
12 large cabbage leaves
1½ pounds ground beef
1 egg
1 medium onion, grated
¼ cup bread crumbs
Salt and pepper to taste
¾ cup water
3 or 4 pieces sour salt
½ cup brown sugar
1 8-ounce can tomato sauce

Pour boiling water over cabbage leaves and allow to sit 2 to 5 minutes, until leaves are soft and pliable.

Mix ground beef, egg, onion, bread crumbs, salt, and pepper; form into balls. Roll each ball into a cabbage leaf.

In the cooker, mix the ¾ cup water, sour salt, brown sugar, and tomato sauce. Place the cabbage balls in the liquid in the cooker, in layers if needed. Close the cooker and place regulator on top. Cook for 30 minutes after regulator rocks gently. Cool at once. Serve.

chinese meatballs

Yield: 4 servings

1 pound ground beef
1½ cups finely grated cabbage
1 large onion, finely grated
½ teaspoon ginger
2 teaspoons soy sauce
½ teaspoon salt
2 tablespoons shortening
½ cup water
1 teaspoon soy sauce

The night before you plan to serve them, mix ground beef, cabbage, onion, ginger, soy sauce, and salt in a large bowl. When thoroughly mixed, form into balls. Cover and set in the refrigerator. (While this can be done when preparing the meal, the flavors blend more fully under refrigeration.)

Heat shortening in cooker and brown the meatballs. Add water and soy sauce and close cover securely. Put pressure control in place. When pressure is reached, cook for 5 minutes. Cool at once under running water.

Serve meatballs with your favorite sweet-and-sour sauce or as is.

porcupine meatballs

Yield: 4 servings

> 1 pound ground beef
> ½ cup uncooked rice
> 1 medium onion, chopped fine
> 1 teaspoon salt
> ¼ teaspoon pepper
> ¾ cup water
> 1 10½-ounce can tomato soup

Mix together ground beef, rice, onion, salt, and pepper. Form into 8 meatballs.
In the cooker, mix water and tomato soup. Drop meatballs into the liquid mixture. Close the cooker and set pressure control in place. When pressure is reached, cook for 8 minutes. Cool cooker naturally for 5 minutes, then place under cold water. Serve.

porcupine meatballs

38

company porcupine meatballs

Yield: 4 servings

    1 pound ground beef
    ½ cup uncooked rice
    1 teaspoon salt
    Dash of pepper
    ⅔ cup tomato puree
    1 onion, cut in rings
    1 cup tomato sauce
    1 cup diced celery
    1 green pepper, diced
    1 teaspoon salt
    ½ teaspoon dry
        mustard
    1 tablespoon sugar
    ¼ cup hot water

Combine ground beef, rice, salt, pepper, and tomato puree in a mixing bowl. Shape into about 8 meatballs.

Place onion, tomato sauce, celery, and green pepper in the cooker.

Mix salt, mustard, and sugar in the hot water.

Place meatballs in the cooker and pour the hot-water mixture over them. Close cover securely, with pressure control in place. When the pressure control is rocking gently, cook for 8 minutes. Cool cooker at once. Serve.

meatballs in raisin sauce

Yield: 4 servings

    1 pound ground beef
    1 onion, minced fine
    ¼ cup crushed corn flakes
    1 egg
    1½ teaspoons salt
    ¼ teaspoon pepper
    1/8 teaspoon paprika
    2 tablespoons shortening
    ½ cup water
    1 tablespoon sugar
    ¼ cup raisins
    2 tablespoons lemon juice

Combine beef, onion, corn flakes, egg, salt, pepper, and paprika. Shape this mixture into 8 meatballs.

Heat the shortening in the cooker and brown the meatballs. Add water, sugar, raisins, and lemon juice. Close cover securely and put pressure control in place. When control is rocking gently, cook for 8 minutes. Cool the cooker at once under cold water. Serve.

meat loaf

meat loaf

Yield: 4 to 6 servings

2 pounds ground beef	½ cup corn flakes
2 teaspoons salt	1 teaspoon Worcestershire
Dash of pepper	sauce
2 eggs, slightly beaten	1 tablespoon shortening
1 onion, minced	½ cup water

Mix ground beef, salt, pepper, eggs, onion, corn flakes, and Worcestershire sauce together well. Shape into a loaf (or 2 small loaves to fit the cooker). Refrigerate in foil for several hours. This prevents loaf from breaking apart while cooking; it may be done the night before, if desired.

Heat shortening in cooker and brown the loaf or loaves on all sides.

Remove loaf from cooker and insert rack. Place meat on rack and add water. Close cover securely and put pressure control in place. When control is rocking gently, cook for 12 to 15 minutes. Cool cooker normally for 5 minutes, then put it under the faucet. Serve.

ham and sweet potatoes

Yield: 4 servings

Whole cloves
¾-inch-thick ham slices to make 4 serving pieces
1 tablespoon fat
2 tablespoons brown sugar
½ cup pineapple juice
½ cup water
2 sweet potatoes, peeled and halved
1 tablespoon cornstarch
2 tablespoons lemon juice

Press cloves into each piece of ham.

Heat fat in cooker and brown the ham. Add brown sugar, pineapple juice, water, and sweet potatoes. Close cover and set pressure control in place. When pressure is reached, cook for 9 minutes. Remove cooker from heat and allow to cool normally for 5 minutes, then place under running water. Set ham and potatoes on a warm platter.

Mix cornstarch and lemon juice and add to liquid in cooker. Stir until clear and slightly thickened.

Pour sauce over ham and sweet potatoes. Serve.

picnic ham

Yield: 6 or more servings

4 pounds ham
10 or more whole cloves
1½ cups pineapple juice
½ cup black raisins

Dot ham with whole cloves. Place ham on rack in pressure cooker. Pour pineapple juice over all. Close cover securely; put pressure regulator in place. When pressure is reached, cook for 30 minutes. Allow pressure to drop of its own accord.

If gravy is desired, thicken the essence slightly and add black raisins. Serve gravy over slices of ham.

lamb stew I

lamb stew I

Yield: 4 to 6 servings

> 2 tablespoons shortening
> 2 pounds breast of lamb, cut
>   in cubes
> Salt and pepper to taste
> 1 green pepper, diced
> 4 onions, diced
> 1 tablespoon Worcestershire
>   sauce
> 4 carrots, cut in half
> ½ cut hot water

Heat shortening in cooker. Brown the lamb thoroughly. Season with salt and pepper. Add green pepper, onions, Worcestershire sauce, carrots, and water. Cover cooker securely and put pressure control in place. When pressure is reached and control jiggling, cook for 15 minutes. Allow the pressure to drop naturally. Serve.

Note: If you want to add potatoes to this stew, add 1 cup diced potatoes with the other vegetables.

42

lamb stew II

Yield: 4 to 6 servings

    1½ **pounds boneless lamb, cut**
        into cubes
    ¼ **cup flour**
    2 tablespoons shortening
    2 onions, sliced
    1 cup tomato puree
    1 teaspoon salt
    ¼ **teaspoon paprika**
    1 cup beef stock
    Parsley for garnish

Dredge lamb in flour.

Heat shortening in cooker and brown the lamb on all sides. Add onions, tomato puree, salt, paprika, and beef stock. Close cover of cooker and put pressure control in place. When pressure is reached, cook for 15 minutes. Allow cooker to cool normally.

Garnish lamb with parsley. Serve on a bed of broad noodles.

moussaka

Yield: 4 servings

    2 tablespoons shortening
    1 pound ground lamb
    1 medium onion, chopped
    1 medium eggplant, pared
        and diced
    3 tablespoons parsley
    1 teaspoon salt
    ¼ **teaspoon paprika**
    ¼ **teaspoon oregano**
    2 whole tomatoes, diced
    ¼ **cup water**
    Grated cheese for garnish

Heat shortening in cooker. Brown the lamb and onion together. Add rest of ingredients in order given. Close cover and set pressure control in place. When pressure is reached, cook for 5 minutes. Cool cooker at once under running water.

Sprinkle moussaka with grated cheese; serve.

moussaka

calf liver with apple and onion rings

Yield: 4 to 6 servings

1 pound calf liver, sliced
¼ cup flour
2 tablespoons shortening
2 medium onions, sliced and
    separated into rings

½ cup water
5 medium apples, peeled, cored,
    and sliced into ¼-inch rings
1 teaspoon salt
½ teaspoon pepper

Dredge liver slices in flour.

Heat shortening in pressure cooker and brown the liver on both sides. Remove liver.

Lightly tan the onions in remaining shortening. Remove from pan.

Put rack in place. Add water. Put liver, onion rings, and apple rings on the rack. Add salt and pepper. Close cover and put pressure control in place. When pressure is reached, cook for 5 minutes. Let pressure drop of its own accord. Serve.

44

pork and pears

Yield: 4 to 6 servings

2 tablespoons shortening	1 teaspoon salt
2 pounds boneless pork loin roast	¼ teaspoon pepper
3 large potatoes, diced	¼ teaspoon dried marjoram
3 large ripe green pears, cut into eighths	¼ teaspoon dillweed
	1½ cups water

Heat shortening in cooker. Brown the meat on all sides. Add the rest of the ingredients in order given. Close cover and put pressure control in place. When pressure is reached, cook for 40 minutes. Allow pressure to drop normally.

Thicken gravy if desired. Serve.

pork chops in cider

Yield: 4 to 6 servings

1 tablespoon shortening	2 apples, pared and diced
4 to 6 pork chops, ½ inch thick	½ teaspoon salt
2 medium onions	Dash of pepper
	½ cup apple cider

Heat shortening in cooker. Brown each pork chop on both sides. Add onions, apples, salt, and pepper; pour apple cider over all. Close cover on cooker and set pressure regulator in place. When pressure is reached, cook for 15 minutes. Cool at once under running water. Serve.

Mashed potatoes and applesauce complete the meal.

pork chops in chili sauce

Yield: 4 servings

2 teaspoons shortening	½ teaspoon salt
4 to 5 pork chops, ½ inch thick	¼ teaspoon lemon pepper
4 to 5 lemon slices	½ cup chili sauce
1 onion, cut in rings	½ cup water

Melt shortening in cooker. Brown the chops on both sides. When browned, place a lemon slice on top of each chop. Add onion and seasonings.

Blend chili sauce with water; pour over chops. Close cover of cooker; put pressure control in place. When pressure is reached, cook for 15 minutes. Cool cooker at once under running water.

Serve the chops in their own gravy.

breaded pork chops

Yield: 5 to 6 servings

    5 to 6 pork chops, ¾ inch thick
    Salt and pepper
    1 teaspoon garlic salt
    1 cup corn-flake crumbs
    1 egg, beaten
    1 tablespoon milk
    3 tablespoons shortening
    ½ cup orange juice

Season chops with salt, pepper, and garlic salt. Dredge in corn flakes and dip in combined egg and milk. Then dredge again in crumbs.

Heat shortening in cooker and brown each chop on both sides. Add orange juice; close cooker. Set pressure control in place and, when pressure is reached, cook for 14 minutes. Allow the pressure to drop naturally. Serve.

pork chops with pineapple

Yield: 4 servings

    4 pork chops, ¾ inch thick
    Salt and pepper
    2 tablespoons shortening
    4 whole pineapple slices
    4 teaspoons brown sugar
    ½ cup pineapple juice
    1 cup sour cream

Season the pork chops with salt and pepper.

Heat the shortening in cooker and brown the chops. On top of each chop lay 1 slice of pineapple, filling the center hole with 1 teaspoon of brown sugar. Add fruit juice. Close cover of cooker and put pressure regulator in place. When pressure is reached, cook for 12 minutes. Allow pressure to drop naturally. Remove chops with fruit in place and set aside.

Add sour cream to the pan juices and serve over the chops.

polynesian pork

Yield: 4 servings

> 2 tablespoons shortening
> 1½ pounds pork, cut into bite-size cubes
> 1 medium onion, sliced
> 1 cup pineapple juice
> ¼ cup vinegar
> ¼ cup brown sugar
> 1 teaspoon salt
> 1 green pepper, diced
> 1 1-pound 4-ounce can pineapple chunks, drained
> 1 cut-up orange
> 1 tablespoon soy sauce
> 3 tablespoons cornstarch
> ¼ cup water

Heat shortening in cooker and brown the pork with the onion. Add pineapple juice, vinegar, brown sugar, and salt. Close cover of cooker and put pressure control in place. When pressure is reached, cook for 12 minutes. Reduce pressure under faucet. Open cooker. Add green pepper, pineapple chunks, orange, and soy sauce.

Mix cornstarch with water and pour into cooker. Stir constantly until slightly thickened.

Serve pork over rice or noodles.

smoked tongue

Yield: About 6 servings

> 3 pounds smoked tongue
> 3 cups water
> 1 whole onion, stuck with 3 cloves
> 6 peppercorns

Soak the smoked tongue in cold water for 2 hours. Drain.

Put tongue on rack in cooker. Add 3 cups water, onion, and peppercorns. Close cover securely and set pressure regulator in place. When pressure is reached, cook for 55 minutes. Allow pressure to drop naturally.

When tongue can be taken from cooker, remove skin.

Strain the liquid and replace tongue in it to retain moisture. Serve.

Picture on next pages: polynesian pork

beef tongue with raisin sauce

Yield: 6 or more servings

3 pounds tongue
2 cups water
1 tablespoon salt
2 or 3 bay leaves
6 peppercorns
1 whole onion, stuck with cloves

Wash tongue and place on rack in cooker. Add the rest of the ingredients and close cover. Set pressure regulator in place. When pressure is reached, cook for 45 minutes. Allow pressure to drop naturally.

When tongue can be removed from cooker, take off the outer skin.

Strain the liquid. Replace skinned tongue in liquid until ready to serve.

raisin sauce

2 tablespoons butter or **1½ cups fruit juice**
margarine **½ cup seedless raisins**
2 tablespoons flour **1 tablespoon sherry wine**

Combine butter and flour in a saucepan, stirring constantly. Add fruit juice and raisins and bring to a boil, stirring all the while. Simmer until thickened, about 10 minutes. Add sherry wine and pour over sliced beef tongue.

beef tongue with raisin sauce

smoked tongue

veal and potatoes

Yield: 4 servings

3 tablespoons shortening
2 pounds veal, cut in
    cubes
1 teaspoon salt

Dash of pepper
1½ cups water
6 medium potatoes, peeled
    and diced

Heat shortening in cooker. Brown the veal cubes in the fat. Add salt, pepper, and water. Close cover securely and set pressure control in place. When pressure is reached and control jiggles, cook for 8 minutes. Allow cooker to cool for 5 minutes, then reduce the rest of pressure under running water.

Open cooker and add potatoes. Again, close cover and put control in place. When pressure is reached, cook for 8 minutes more. Reduce pressure at once under running water. Serve.

veal birds

Yield: 4 servings

    1½ pounds veal steak,
       ½ inch thick
    2 cups of your favorite
       bread stuffing
    ¼ pound bacon, sliced
    Flour
    Salt and pepper to taste
    2 tablespoons shortening
    ½ cup water

veal birds

Cut steak into serving pieces. Place a tablespoon of stuffing on the center of each portion. (Try some stuffed olives in that stuffing. Mmmmm, good.) Roll up the veal and wrap with 1 slice of bacon. Tie with string or use a skewer. Roll the veal in flour seasoned with salt and pepper.

Heat shortening in cooker. Brown the veal birds on all sides. Add water. Close cover and set pressure regulator in place. When regulator rocks gently, cook for 10 minutes. Let pressure drop of its own accord. Serve.

veal fricassee

Yield: 4 servings

    1½ pounds veal steak, ½ inch thick
    1 teaspoon salt
    Dash of pepper
    3 tablespoons flour
    2 tablespoons shortening
    1 tablespoon chopped onion
    1 teaspoon paprika
    1 bouillon cube
    ¾ cup water
    1 cup sour cream

Cut veal into serving pieces and season well with salt and pepper. Dredge in flour.

Put shortening in cooker. Brown the onion and veal steak in hot fat. Add paprika.

Dissolve the bouillon cube in water and pour over meat. Cover the cooker and set pressure control in place. When pressure is reached, cook for 15 minutes. Cool normally for 5 minutes, then place under running water. Remove cover. Add sour cream, stirring in until blended.

Serve fricassee with noodles or rice.

veal balls with dill

Yield: 4 servings

2 slices white bread, soaked in milk and squeezed
½ onion, chopped fine
1 egg
1 pound ground veal
1 teaspoon salt
Dash of pepper
¼ cup flour
2 tablespoons shortening
½ cup beef broth
1 tablespoon dillweed
½ cup sour cream

Mix bread, onion, egg, and meat in a bowl. Add salt and pepper. Form meat mixture into balls. Roll each ball in flour to coat it.

Heat shortening in cooker and brown the meatballs on all sides. Add beef broth. Close cooker and set pressure control in place. When pressure is reached, cook for 5 minutes. Cool cooker at once under running water.

Mix dillweed and sour cream and heat in cooker until meat and liquid are all well-blended. Serve.

This dish goes nicely with mashed potatoes to absorb the good gravy.

your own favorite meat recipe

Yield: 4 to 6 servings

This page is left blank for you. If you have read this much about pressure cooking, you should be ready to adapt one of your own favorites to the ease and speed of pressure cooking. Have fun.

chicken breasts in wine

Yield: 4 to 6 servings

2 to 3 pounds chicken breasts
¼ cup flour
Salt and pepper to taste
½ teaspoon garlic salt
2 tablespoons shortening
½ cup red wine

Dredge the chicken in mixture of flour, salt, pepper, and garlic salt.

Heat the shortening in the cooker and brown the chicken in it. Add wine; close cover. Put valve on cooker. After pressure is reached and valve is slowly rocking, cook for 10 minutes. Allow the cooker to cool naturally. Serve.

rolled chicken breasts

rolled chicken breasts

Yield: 6 servings

2 tablespoons melted butter
    or margarine
½ teaspoon salt
¼ cup bread crumbs
2 tablespoons finely
    chopped celery
1 tablespoon finely chopped onion
1 tablespoon parsley
3 whole chicken breasts, boned
    and halved
2 tablespoons cooking oil
1 cup water

In a fry pan mix melted butter, salt, bread crumbs, celery, onion, and parsley to make the stuffing.

Put chicken pieces skin-side-down. Put some of the stuffing mixture in the center of each piece. Roll the chicken over the stuffing and fasten together with skewers.

Heat cooking oil in pressure cooker. Brown each piece of chicken. Add water; close cover of cooker. Set pressure control in place. When pressure is reached, cook for 10 minutes. Cool at once under running water. Serve.

chicken oriental

Yield: 4 to 6 servings

> 2 tablespoons shortening
> 3 chicken breasts, boned, halved, and skinned
> Salt and pepper to taste
> ½ cup sliced water chestnuts
> 1 green pepper, chopped
> 1 tablespoon ginger
> ¼ cup sugar
> 1 tablespoon soy sauce
> ½ cup pineapple juice
> ½ cup wine vinegar
> 1 cup drained, crushed pineapple
> 2 tablespoons cornstarch
> ¼ cup water

Heat shortening in cooker.

Season chicken breasts with salt and pepper. Brown them in the cooker. Add water chestnuts, green pepper, and ginger.

Dissolve the sugar in soy sauce, juice, and vinegar. (Add extra sugar if preferred.) Add to the chicken. Last, put pineapple over chicken and close cooker. Set pressure control in place. When pressure is reached, cook for 10 minutes. Cool at once under running water. Return open cooker to low flame.

Dissolve the cornstarch in water. Add to the chicken, stirring until liquid is slightly thickened.

Serve chicken over rice or buttered noodles.

boned chicken in tarragon

Yield: 6 servings

> 3 whole chicken breasts, boned,
>   halved, and skinned
> Salt and pepper
> ¼ cup flour
> 2 tablespoons shortening
> 1 tablespoon chopped onion
> ½ teaspoon tarragon
> ½ cup white wine
> ¼ cup heavy cream

After seasoning the chicken with salt and pepper, dredge it in flour. Set aside.

Heat shortening in the cooker and brown the onion. Add tarragon, wine, and chicken. Close cover. Put pressure control in place. When pressure is reached, cook 10 minutes. Cool cooker at once under running water. Remove chicken to a warm platter.

Add cream to cooker, stirring to blend flavors.

Pour the sauce over chicken. Serve.

iranian chicken and rice

Yield: 4 to 6 servings

2 whole boned chicken breasts, skinned and cut in serving pieces
1 cup rice
1 orange, halved, sliced with rind left on

1 lemon, halved, sliced with rind left on
½ cup slivered almonds
½ cup raisins
1 teaspoon salt
1 cup orange juice

Place ingredients in cooker in order given. Close cover and put pressure regulator in place. When pressure is reached, cook for 10 minutes. Allow to cool normally. Stir gently just once. Serve.

chicken teriyaki

Yield: 4 to 6 servings

3 to 4 pounds chicken parts
Teriyaki sauce to cover the chicken
½ cup water

Marinate the chicken parts in the teriyaki sauce for at least 1 hour.
Place the chicken and marinade in the cooker. Add the water. Close cover securely and put the pressure control in place. When pressure is reached, cook for 15 to 20 minutes, depending on age of the chicken. Allow to cool naturally. Serve.

chicken and bananas

Yield: 4 to 6 servings

2- to 3-pound chicken, cut into serving pieces
Salt and pepper
2 tablespoons shortening
½ cup water
3 or 4 bananas, cut lengthwise and quartered

Season chicken with salt and pepper.
Heat shortening in cooker and brown the chicken. Add water and bananas. Close cover and put pressure control in place. When pressure is reached, cook for 15 minutes. Allow cooker to cool of its own accord.
Serve chicken and bananas with a fresh-fruit salad and homemade bread.

battered chicken

Yield: 4 to 6 servings

¼ **cup flour**
Salt and pepper
½ **teaspoon paprika**
2 **to 3 pounds chicken, cut into serving pieces**
2 **tablespoons shortening**
½ **cup water**

Mix flour, salt, pepper, and paprika together. Roll each piece of chicken in this.

Heat the cooker and add the shortening. Brown the battered chicken. Add water and close cover securely. Put regulator on vent pipe. When the pressure is reached and regulator rocking slowly, time the chicken. Cook 10 to 15 minutes. Allow to cool naturally, about 10 minutes.

If you want a gravy, thicken the essence to desired consistency. Serve.

chicken curry

Yield: 4 to 6 servings

2 **tablespoons shortening**
3 **pounds chicken, cut into serving pieces**
2 **teaspoons curry powder**
2 **teaspoons salt**
2 **onions, chopped**
1 **teaspoon vinegar**
1 **cup water**
2 **tablespoons cornstarch**
¼ **cup orange juice**

Heat shortening in cooker. Brown the chicken. Add curry powder, salt, onions, vinegar, and water. Close cover of cooker and set pressure regulator in place. When pressure is reached, cook for 10 minutes. Cool cooker at once under faucet. Set chicken aside to keep warm.

Combine cornstarch and orange juice; stir into remaining liquid in cooker.

When thickened, pour over the chicken and serve with boiled rice.

chicken with dill

Yield: 4 to 6 servings

¼ **cup flour**
Salt and pepper to taste
1 **teaspoon dillweed**
2 **to 3 pounds chicken, cut into serving pieces**
2 **tablespoons shortening**
½ **cup water**

Combine flour, salt, pepper, and dillweed. Coat the chicken with flour mixture.

Melt shortening in cooker. Brown the chicken. Add water and close cover securely. Place valve on cooker. When pressure is reached, cook for 10 to 15 minutes. Allow to cool of its own accord.

Thicken gravy if desired. Serve.

chicken in fruit sauce

chicken in fruit sauce

Yield: 4 to 6 servings

2- to 3-pound chicken, cut into serving pieces
Salt and pepper to taste
2 tablespoons shortening

1 cup orange juice
¼ cup honey
2 tablespoons lemon juice
½ teaspoon ground curry powder

Season the chicken pieces with salt and pepper.

Heat shortening in cooker. Brown the chicken on all sides. Add orange juice, honey, lemon juice, and curry powder. Close cover of cooker and set pressure regulator in place. When pressure is reached, cook for 15 minutes. Let pressure drop of its own accord.

Remove chicken from cooker and arrange in baking dish. Surround with your choice of fruit—peaches, pears, apricots, etc.

Pour sauce over the chicken and fruit and put under the broiler for 5 minutes or until fruit is hot. Serve.

chicken hawaiian

Since this is good enough for a party, chicken breasts and legs are preferred.

Yield: 4 to 6 servings

 3 pounds chicken, cut into serving pieces
 Flour to dredge chicken
 2 tablespoons shortening
 1 teaspoon salt
 Dash of pepper
 1 cup pineapple juice
 ¼ teaspoon ground cloves
 ¼ teaspoon nutmeg
 ½ cup pineapple tidbits
 ½ cup slivered almonds (optional)

Dredge the chicken pieces in flour and set aside.

Place shortening in pressure cooker and add chicken. Brown each piece. Add salt, pepper, pineapple juice, cloves, and nutmeg. Close cover and set pressure control in place. When pressure is reached and control jiggles, cook for 10 minutes. Cool at once under running water.

Add pineapple tidbits and almonds and heat through.

Serve chicken on rice with an Aloha.

chicken with olives

Yield: 4 to 6 servings

2 tablespoons shortening
2- to 3-pound chicken, cut into
    serving pieces
1 medium onion,
    chopped
1 carrot, diced
1 or 2 tomatoes, peeled
    and quartered
2 tablespoons tomato puree
24 green olives, pitted and
    chopped fine
½ cup water

Heat shortening in cooker. Brown chicken pieces. Add the rest of the ingredients in order given. Close cover of cooker and put pressure control in place. When pressure is reached, cook for 10 minutes. Allow pressure to drop naturally. Serve.

chicken hawaiian

chicken paprika

Yield: 4 to 6 servings

   2- to 3-pound chicken, cut into
        serving pieces
   1 teaspoon salt
   1 teaspoon garlic salt
   Dash of pepper
   1 teaspoon paprika
   ¼ cup flour
   3 tablespoons shortening
   1 cup water
   1 cup sour cream

Dredge the chicken in a mixture of salt, garlic salt, pepper, paprika, and flour.
Heat shortening in cooker. Brown the chicken. Add water; close cover securely. Set pressure control in place. When pressure is reached, cook for 20 minutes. Cool cooker normally for 5 minutes, then reduce pressure under faucet.
Last, stir in the sour cream, heating thoroughly. Serve.

chicken paprika

chicken in peanut sauce

Yield: 4 to 6 servings

2 to 3 pounds chicken, cut into serving pieces
1 large onion, sliced
2 tablespoons shortening
3 tomatoes, chopped
¼ cup tomato paste
1 teaspoon salt
Dash of pepper
½ cup water
½ cup chunky peanut butter

In the cooker, brown chicken and onion in shortening. Add tomatoes, tomato paste, salt, pepper, and water. Close cover and put pressure regulator in place. When pressure is reached, cook for 15 minutes. Allow pressure to drop normally. Open cooker.

Remove some of the hot liquid from the chicken and mix with the chunky peanut butter. Pour this sauce over the chicken. Simmer and stir for 2 minutes. Serve.

persian chicken

Yield: 4 servings

2 tablespoons shortening
1 onion, finely chopped
2- to 3-pound chicken, cut into serving pieces
1 cup chopped walnuts
4 tablespoons lemon juice
1 to 2 teaspoons sugar
2 cups water

Heat shortening in cooker. Lightly tan the onion. Add chicken pieces, walnuts, lemon juice, sugar, and water. Close cover of cooker and set pressure control in place. When pressure is reached, cook for 20 to 25 minutes, depending on age of chicken. Let pressure drop naturally.

Serve chicken over rice.

chicken pilau

Yield: 4 to 6 servings

1 cup rice
4 stalks celery, diced
1 large onion, quartered
1 large green pepper, chopped
3 tomatoes, chopped
1 cup chicken broth
2 cups diced cooked chicken
6 strips cooked bacon, broken into pieces

Place rice, celery, onion, green pepper, tomatoes, and chicken broth into cooker. Close cover and put pressure control in place. When pressure is reached and control jiggles gently, remove cooker from flame. Allow pressure to reduce normally.

Return open cooker to low flame. Add chicken and bacon. Simmer for 3 minutes, stirring to mix the flavors.

Serve chicken hot.

chicken in the pot

Yield: 4 to 6 servings

2- to 3-pound chicken, cut into serving pieces	2 tablespoons salt
¼ cup flour	¼ teaspoon fresh ground pepper
2 tablespoons shortening	½ teaspoon garlic salt
1 bay leaf	1 cup diced carrots
2 tablespoons minced onion	1 cup fresh peas
	½ cup water

Dredge chicken pieces in flour.

Heat shortening in cooker and brown the chicken. Add seasonings, vegetables, and water. Close cover and set pressure regulator in place. When pressure is reached, cook for 10 minutes. Allow pressure to drop naturally.

Serve chicken with buttered noodles.

chicken and sausage

Yield: 4 to 6 servings

½ pound link sausage	1 onion, minced
2- to 3-pound chicken, cut into serving pieces	2 cups tomatoes, drained
	½ cup water

Brown the sausage in cooker; pour off excess fat. Set sausage aside.

Brown the chicken in 2 tablespoons of sausage fat. Add onion, tomatoes, water, and sausage. Close cover securely and put pressure control in place. When pressure is reached, cook for 10 minutes. Allow the pressure to drop normally.

Enjoy the delicious combination of chicken and sausage.

spanish chicken

Yield: 4 to 6 servings

2- to 3-pound chicken, cut into serving pieces	3 red or green peppers, diced
Salt and pepper	¼ pound ham, diced
2 tablespoons shortening	3 tomatoes, chopped
1 onion, sliced	½ cup water
1 garlic clove, minced	12 green olives with pimientos, halved

Season chicken pieces with salt and pepper; brown them in shortening. Add onion, garlic, peppers, ham, tomatoes, and water. Close cover of cooker and put pressure control in place. When pressure is reached, cook for 15 minutes. Allow pressure to drop normally.

Return open cooker to a low flame. Add the olives and simmer for 2 minutes.

Serve chicken with **seasoned rice.**

stewed chicken

stewed chicken

Yield: 4 servings

3 pounds stewing chicken, cut
    into serving pieces
2 cups water
2 teaspoons salt

3 peppercorns
2 ribs celery with leaves
1 sliced carrot
1 medium-size onion, quartered

Place all ingredients in the pressure cooker in the order given. Close cover and set pressure regulator in place. When pressure is reached, cook for 25 minutes. Let pressure drop of its own accord.

If gravy is desired, remove chicken from the liquid and strain the liquid. Then thicken liquid to make gravy. Replace chicken to heat it thoroughly.

Serve chicken at once.

chicken sub gum

Yield: 4 to 6 servings

2 cups chicken, cooked and cut
    into pieces
2 cups shredded cabbage
1 cup diced green pepper
1 cup diced celery
1 cup chicken broth
1 tablespoon cornstarch

3 tablespoons soy sauce
2 tablespoons dark molasses
1 teaspoon salt
1 teaspoon vinegar
¼ cup water
2 tomatoes, cubed
½ cup blanched almonds

Combine chicken, cabbage, green pepper, celery, and chicken broth in cooker. Close cover and set pressure control in place. When pressure is reached, cook for 2 minutes. Cool at once under running water.

Mix cornstarch, soy sauce, molasses, salt, and vinegar in water. Add to the chicken and vegetables, stirring gently. When mixture has thickened, add tomatoes and ¼ cup almonds. Cook for 1 minute more.

Sprinkle remaining almonds on top and serve with rice.

easy chicken supreme

Yield: 4 to 6 servings

2 to 3 pounds chicken, cut into serving pieces	2 tablespoons shortening
¼ cup flour	1 package onion soup mix
	½ cup water

Dredge chicken pieces in flour.

Heat shortening in cooker and brown the chicken. Add onion soup mix and water. Close cover of cooker and set pressure regulator in place. When pressure is reached and regulator jiggling gently, cook for 15 minutes. Allow pressure to drop of its own accord.

Thicken gravy, if desired, and you have a supremely good dish.

chicken tarragon

Yield: 4 to 6 servings

2 to 3 pounds chicken, cut into serving pieces
¼ cup fresh tarragon leaves or 2 tablespoons dried tarragon
4 green onions, minced
1 cup dry white wine
2 tablespoons shortening
1 tablespoon lemon juice
Parsley for garnish

Marinate the chicken in tarragon, onions, and wine for 1 hour. Remove chicken, reserving liquid.

Heat shortening in pressure cooker. Brown the chicken on all sides. Add marinade and lemon juice. Close cover and set pressure control in place. When pressure is reached, cook for 15 minutes. Let pressure drop of its own accord.

Garnish chicken with parsley and serve.

chicken in tomato sauce

Yield: 4 to 6 servings

2- to 3-pound chicken, cut into serving pieces	2 tablespoons chopped green onion
Salt	½ cup catsup
2 tablespoons shortening	½ cup water
1 tablespoon dillweed	

Rub the chicken pieces with salt.

Heat shortening in cooker and brown the chicken on all sides. Sprinkle with dillweed and onion; add catsup and water. Close cover of cooker and set pressure regulator in place. When pressure is reached, cook for 15 minutes. Allow cooker to cool of its own accord. Serve.

sautéed chicken liver

Yield: 6 to 8 servings

2 slices bacon
2 pounds chicken liver, halved
¼ cup sliced onions
¼ cup sliced mushrooms
1 teaspoon salt
Dash of pepper
½ cup water

Crisp-fry the bacon in the pressure cooker. Remove the bacon and set aside.

Sauté the chicken liver and onions in the bacon fat. Pour off any excess fat. Add the remaining ingredients. Close cover and set pressure regulator in place. When pressure is reached, cook for 5 minutes. Cool at once under running water.

Serve the chicken livers on a bed of rice and sprinkle with the crumbled bacon bits.

rock cornish hens

Yield: 2 to 4 servings

2 Rock Cornish hens
Salt and pepper
2 teaspoons crumbled tarragon leaves
3 tablespoons cooking oil
1 onion, diced
½ cup diced carrots
1 cup diced celery
1 tablespoon chopped parsley
1 bay leaf
4 tomatoes, peeled and quartered
½ cup white wine

Sprinkle the hens amply with salt and pepper. Put the tarragon leaves in the cavities, for flavor.

Heat the oil in the cooker and tan the onion lightly. Brown the hens and remove.

Combine carrots, celery, rest of seasonings, and tomatoes with the tanned onions. Put the hens back in cooker and pour wine over them. Close cover and set regulator in place. When pressure is reached, cook 8 minutes. Allow to cool normally.

Remove hens and put on a warming platter.

Thicken gravy if desired.

Serve hens with wild rice.

cornish hens in sweet sauce

Yield: 2 to 4 servings

2 Rock Cornish hens
Salt and pepper
2 tablespoons shortening
½ cup raisins
2 teaspoons lemon juice
½ teaspoon allspice
½ cup chicken broth
½ cup red currant jelly

Sprinkle the hens amply with salt and pepper.

Heat shortening in pressure cooker and brown the hens. Add raisins, lemon juice, allspice, and chicken broth. Close cover and set pressure regulator in place. When pressure is reached, cook for 8 minutes. Allow to cool normally.

Remove hens and blend jelly with the sauce in cooker, stirring constantly. Brush the sauce over the hens.

To crisp them, put hens under a broiler for 2 minutes. Serve.

stuffed hens hawaiian

Yield: 2 to 4 servings

2 tablespoons butter or margarine
¼ cup hot water
¼ cup packaged stuffing mix
1 egg, slightly beaten
¼ cup drained crushed pineapple
2 tablespoons finely chopped nuts (macadamia for the true Hawaiian)
2 Cornish hens
2 tablespoons shortening
½ teaspoon salt
Dash of pepper
1 cup pineapple juice

Melt butter in hot water. Stir in stuffing, egg, pineapple, and nuts. Stuff the hens with this mixture.

Heat shortening in cooker and brown the hens. Add salt, pepper, and pineapple juice. Close cover and set pressure control in place. When pressure is reached and control jiggles, cook for 8 minutes. Cool cooker at once under running water.

If desired, place hens under broiler until crisp. Serve.

carp in red wine

Yield: 6 servings

3 pounds carp, dressed
Salt and pepper to taste
1 medium onion, chopped
1 tablespoon parsley
1 teaspoon dillseed
3 whole peppercorns
½ cup red wine

Season the fish with salt and pepper, then wrap it in cheesecloth to prevent fish from falling apart when removed from cooker. Place the wrapped fish in pressure cooker. Add rest of ingredients. Close cover of cooker and set pressure control in place. When pressure is reached, cook for 8 minutes. Cool cooker at once under running water. Drain carp and remove cheesecloth.

Serve fish on a platter with lemon slices.

carp in red wine

scandinavian cod

Yield: 6 to 8 servings

2 pounds codfish, cut into
    serving pieces
2 cups water
1 teaspoon salt
6 tablespoons butter or margarine

¼ cup flour
1 teaspoon salt
1 teaspoon dry mustard
2½ cups cream

Place fish, water, and salt in pressure cooker. Close cover and set pressure control in place. When control is rocking gently, cook for 1 minute. Reduce pressure at once under running water. Set aside fish to keep warm.

Melt butter and add flour, salt, and mustard. Stirring constantly, add cream until mixture is thickened. Place the fish in this sauce and be sure it is heated through.

Small, boiled potatoes complement this tasty dish.

fresh cod in wine

Yield: 4 servings

4 cod fillets
2 tablespoons shortening
1 finely chopped onion
1 crushed clove garlic

¼ cup chopped parsley
3 tomatoes, peeled and
    quartered
½ cup dry white wine

Wrap fillets in cheesecloth if desired.

Heat shortening in cooker and tan the onion and garlic lightly. Put rack in cooker. Add rest of ingredients around the fish. Last, pour the wine over all. Close cover of cooker and put pressure control in place. When pressure is reached, cook for 4 minutes. Cool at once under running water.

Suggestion for serving: Arrange fish on a platter. Thicken the gravy, if desired, or dot the fish with butter and a shake of paprika. A slice of lemon has both eye- and taste-appeal.

flounder with blue-cheese sauce

Yield: 6 servings

2 pounds flounder fillets
1 tablespoon lemon juice
2 teaspoons minced onion
1 teaspoon minced parsley

¼ cup water
½ cup cream
⅓ cup blue cheese,
    crumbled fine

Lay flounder fillets in bottom of pressure cooker. Add lemon juice, onion, parsley, and water. Close cover and put pressure regulator in place. When regulator rocks gently, cook for 5 minutes. Cool cooker at once under running water.

When you have removed regulator and cover, stir in the cream and blue cheese over a very low flame. When this mixture is heated through, serve at once.

halibut steaks

Yield: 4 or more servings

2 pounds halibut steaks, about 2 inches thick
1 teaspoon salt
3 peppercorns
1 cup tomato juice
½ teaspoon sugar
1 medium-size onion, quartered
½ cup heavy cream

Wrap steaks in cheesecloth.

Put salt, peppercorns, tomato juice, sugar, and onion into cooker. Add the wrapped steaks. Close cover and set pressure control in place. When pressure is reached, cook for 10 minutes. Cool at once under running water. Remove fish and set on a warming platter.

Add heavy cream to the remaining juice and heat thoroughly.

Pour sauce over the fish, and serve.

halibut steaks

fine finnan haddie

Yield: 6 servings

Salt and pepper to taste
2 pounds haddock fillets
1 3-ounce can sliced mushrooms
¼ cup chopped onions
2 tablespoons butter or margarine
4 slices cooked bacon
½ cup water

With heavy-duty aluminum foil form a bowl to fit inside the pressure cooker.
Salt and pepper the fillets and layer them in the bowl.
Sauté the mushrooms and onions in butter and pour the mixture over the fish.
Top with the crumbled bacon bits.
Set water, rack, and foil bowl in the cooker. Close cover securely and set pressure control in place. When pressure is reached, cook for 10 minutes. Cool at once under running water.
Garnish with lemon wedges and parsley, if desired.

dill perch

dill perch

Yield: 4 to 6 servings

2 pounds perch fillets, cut into
serving pieces
4 medium onions, sliced
into rings
1 stalk celery, chopped
2 teaspoons salt
½ cup water
1 cup sour cream
2 dill pickles, chopped
4 teaspoons horseradish
1 teaspoon parsley flakes
Fresh chopped dill for garnish

Put perch, onions, celery, salt, and water in cooker. Close cover and set pressure control in place. When pressure is reached, cook for 3 minutes. Allow cooker to cool normally.
Return open cooker to a low flame. Add sour cream, pickles, horseradish, and parsley flakes. Stir until well-blended and hot.
Garnish perch with dillweed, and serve.

perch

Yield: 4 servings

2 pounds perch
¼ cup flour
2 tablespoons shortening

Salt and pepper
 to taste
½ cup water

Thoroughly coat the fish in flour.

Add shortening to cooker and brown the fish on all sides. Remove from cooker.

Place rack in cooker and put perch on rack. Season with salt and pepper. Add water and close cooker. Put regulator in place and, when pressure is reached, cook for 10 minutes. Cool cooker at once. Serve.

pike in horseradish sauce

Yield: 4 to 6 servings

2 pounds pike
Salt and pepper to taste
½ cup white wine

sauce

1 can cream of celery soup
3 tablespoons horseradish
1 teaspoon sugar
1 teaspoon dry mustard
Lemon slices

Season fish with salt and pepper. Wrap in cheesecloth.

Put rack in cooker. Place fish on rack and pour wine over it. Close cover and put pressure control in place. When pressure is reached, cook for 4 minutes. Cool cooker at once under running water. Remove fish to a heated platter.

To the liquid left in cooker add cream soup (undiluted), horseradish, sugar, and mustard. Stir until all are heated. Pour over the fish.

Garnish fish with lemon slices. Serve.

salmon steaks in dill sauce

Yield: 6 servings

1 tablespoon butter or
 margarine
2 teaspoons finely chopped onion
6 salmon steaks, ½ inch thick

3 tablespoons lemon juice
½ teaspoon dillseed
¼ cup water
½ cup sour cream

Heat butter in cooker and lightly brown the onion. Arrange the steaks in the cooker. Add the lemon juice, dillseed, and water. Close the cooker and set pressure regulator in place. When pressure is reached, cook for 10 minutes. Cool at once. Remove the salmon steaks from the cooker.

To the liquid left in the cooker, mix in the sour cream, stirring constantly. When this sauce has thickened slightly, pour it over the salmon steaks; serve at once.

Picture on next page: perch

salmon ring mold

Yield: 4 servings

> 2 cups cooked or canned salmon
> 2 eggs, well-beaten
> 1 cup milk
> Salt and pepper to taste
> 1 teaspoon chopped parsley
> 1 cup cracker crumbs

Remove dark skin and bones from the salmon and flake into bite-size pieces.

In a mixing bowl add to the salmon the rest of ingredients in order given. Mix well.

Grease a 3-cup ring mold. (Check to make sure the mold will set on the rack in your pressure cooker.) Pack the salmon mixture into the mold and cover with silver foil.

Put 2 cups water in the cooker and set rack in place. Put covered mold on the rack. Close cover and put pressure control in place. When pressure is reached, cook for 10 minutes. Cool cooker at once.

Unmold salmon ring onto serving platter.

salmon loaf

Yield: 4 to 6 servings

> 1 16-ounce can salmon
> 1½ cups soft bread crumbs
> 2 stalks celery, diced fine
> 2 tablespoons minced onion
> 2 eggs, beaten
> 1 can cream of mushroom soup
> ½ cup water
> Lemon slices for garnish

Remove skin and bones from salmon.

Mix salmon, bread crumbs, celery, onion, eggs, and soup in a bowl. Put mixture in a greased casserole dish that will fit into the cooker. (Make a dish out of foil if necessary.)

Put rack in cooker. Add water. Set salmon on rack. Close cover and put pressure regulator in place. When pressure is reached, cook for 20 minutes. Let cool naturally.

If desired, dot the loaf with butter and put under the broiler for 2 minutes, or until butter melts.

Garnish with lemon slices, and serve with fresh peas and a tossed salad.

stuffed red snapper

Yield: 4 to 6 servings

> 1 3- to 4-pound red snapper,
>   cleaned
> Salt
> 4 tablespoons butter or margarine
> ½ small onion, minced
> 1 cup stale bread crumbs
> ½ cup fine cracker crumbs
> ½ teaspoon dill
> 2 teaspoons chopped parsley
> ¼ teaspoon salt
> Pepper to taste
> ½ cup grapefruit juice

Sprinkle the fish with salt inside and out and set aside.

Combine in the cooker the butter, onion, bread and cracker crumbs, dill, parsley, salt, and pepper. When thoroughly mixed, use this stuffing to stuff the fish. Close with string and wrap the fish in cheesecloth.

Put the rack in the cooker. Place stuffed fish on the rack and pour grapefruit juice over it. Close cover and put pressure control in place. When pressure is reached, cook for 8 to 10 minutes. Cool cooker at once. Serve.

white fish and bananas

Any fish will do for this recipe, but white fish is particularly good.

Yield: 4 to 6 servings

> 2 pounds white fish
> Olive oil
> Salt and pepper
> 2 bananas
> 2 tablespoons tomato paste
> 2 tablespoons sugar
> ½ cup water

Split the fish. Brush over it with olive oil. Add salt and pepper to taste.

Split the bananas lengthwise and lay on top of the fish. (Wrap fish in cheesecloth for ease in handling.) Place fish on rack in cooker.

Mix tomato paste, sugar, and water; pour over the fish. Close cover and put pressure control in place. When pressure is reached, cook for 7 minutes. Allow pressure to drop naturally. Serve.

fish creole

Yield: 4 to 6 servings

2 pounds fish fillets
1 No. 2½ can tomatoes
1 teaspoon salt
½ cup green pepper, chopped
6 green olives, chopped
1 tablespoon onion, minced
2 peppercorns

Wrap fillets in cheesecloth to keep the fish from falling apart.

Put rest of ingredients into the cooker in order given. Place rack in cooker and place fish on rack. Close cover and set pressure regulator in place. When pressure is reached, cook for 7 minutes. Allow pressure to drop naturally. Remove fish and put on a warm platter.

Thicken sauce, if desired, and pour over fish. Serve at once.

fish with sauerkraut

Yield: 4 to 6 servings

2 pounds fish fillets, cut into 2-inch pieces
1 medium onion, sliced
1 carrot, diced
1 pound sauerkraut, drained
3 strips bacon, crisply fried and broken up
1 whole tomato, peeled and quartered
1 teaspoon salt
½ cup water
1 cup sour cream
Grated Parmesan cheese

Place fish, onion, carrot, sauerkraut, bacon, tomato, salt, and water into the cooker. Stir gently once to mix together. Close cover of cooker. Put pressure control in place. When pressure is reached, cook 7 minutes. Cool at once under running water.

Return the open cooker to low flame and gradually add sour cream, stirring constantly.

Serve topped with grated Parmesan cheese.

fish fillets with shrimp

fish fillets with shrimp

Yield: 4 to 6 servings

> **2 pounds fillets (flounder is tasty)**
> **Salt and pepper to taste**
> **½ cup water**
> **2 tablespoons butter or margarine**
> **½ pound small cooked shrimp**
> **Lemon wedges**

Season the fillets with salt and pepper and wrap in cheesecloth.

Put water in cooker and set rack in place. Put fish on rack and close cover. Set pressure control in place. When pressure is reached, cook for 10 minutes. Cool at once under running water.

Melt the butter in a saucepan. Toss the shrimp in the butter so that each one becomes coated with butter.

Place the shrimp down the center of each fillet, pour browned butter over the fillets, and serve.

stuffed fish

Yield: 6 servings

stuffing

1½ cups bread crumbs
2 tablespoons melted butter or
    margarine
2 tablespoons chopped onion
¼ cup chopped celery
¼ cup diced green pepper

1 egg, beaten
Salt and pepper to taste

1 3-pound fish (your choice),
    cleaned, scaled, and
    eviscerated
½ cup white wine

Mix the stuffing ingredients together. Stuff the fish lightly. Wrap the fish in cheesecloth.

Put rack in cooker and set fish on rack. Pour white wine over the fish. Close cover. Set pressure control in place and, when pressure is reached, cook for 8 minutes. Cool pressure cooker at once under running water. Serve.

fillet of fish in wine

Yield: 4 servings

2 tablespoons butter or
    margarine
1 pound of fish fillets (sole,
    halibut, pike, or haddock)

Salt and pepper to taste
¾ cup white wine
2 tablespoons lemon juice
2 tablespoons parsley

Melt butter in pressure cooker.

Sprinkle the fish fillets with salt and pepper, then put them into pressure cooker.

Combine remaining ingredients and pour over the fillets. Close cover and set pressure control in place. When pressure is reached, cook for 8 minutes. Cool at once under running water.

If sauce is desired, thicken the liquid left in cooker and pour it over the fillets. Serve.

seafood a la king

Yield: 4 to 6 servings

2 pounds fish fillets, cut into
    1-inch pieces
1 cup chopped celery
1 cup peeled and diced eggplant
1 cup diced cucumber

1 teaspoon salt
Dash of pepper
½ cup water
1 can cream of mushroom soup

Put fish, celery, eggplant, cucumber, salt, pepper, and water in cooker. Close cover securely and put pressure control in place. When pressure is reached, cook 3 minutes. Reduce pressure at once under running water.

Return open cooker to low flame. Add undiluted can of soup, stirring gently to blend and heat.

Serve fish over toast, if desired.

clams steamed in beer

Yield: Depends on how many clams you steam

Soft-shell or little-neck clams
½ cup beer

This is the time to remember *not* to fill the pressure cooker over two-thirds full. Try 2 pounds of clams for starters. Wash clams thoroughly to remove all sand.

Put beer in cooker and set rack in place. Put clams on the rack. Close the cooker and set pressure regulator in place. When pressure is reached, cook for 3 minutes. Cool the cooker at once under faucet.

Reserve the clam liquid to serve with the clams, if desired. Serve.

company king crab

Yield: 10 servings

**¼ cup butter or
    margarine**
**3 pounds king-crab meat, in
    bite-size chunks**
½ cup chopped spring onions

Salt and pepper to taste
¼ cup water
1 cup cream
¼ cup buttered bread crumbs
¼ cup grated cheddar cheese

Melt butter in cooker. Add crab meat and onions, stirring until onions are lightly sautéed. Add salt, pepper, and water. Close cover of cooker and set pressure control in place. When pressure is reached, cook for 2 minutes. Cool cooker at once. Add cream to the hot mixture.

Turn crab mixture into a well-greased baking dish. Top with bread crumbs and cheese mixed together. Place under the broiler until topping forms a crust. Serve.

lobster stew

Yield: 3 to 4 servings

2 to 3 pounds lobster
Boiling water
2 teaspoons salt
1 cup water
3 tablespoons butter

**Enough cream to bring liquid
    to 4 cups**
2 teaspoons onion juice
**Salt and pepper
    to taste**

Put live lobster in boiling water to cover. Remove lobster.

Put salt and water in cooker. Place lobster on rack in cooker. Close cover and set pressure control in place. When pressure is reached, cook for 5 minutes. Cool cooker at once under running water.

Drain lobster and reserve liquid. Pick out the lobster meat in bite-size pieces.

Melt butter in open cooker. Coat lobster meat with butter. Add 4 cups liquid, and onion juice. Bring to a boil and simmer for 2 minutes. Add salt and pepper to taste, and serve.

scallops

Yield: 4 servings

2 tablespoons shortening
1 clove garlic, split
1 pound scallops

1 teaspoon salt
Fresh ground pepper to taste
1 cup dry white wine

Heat shortening and garlic for 2 minutes. Remove garlic—the flavor will remain.

Put rack in cooker. Add scallops and seasonings. Pour wine over scallops. Close cover and put pressure control in place. When pressure is reached, remove from heat. Cool cooker at once under running water.

Serve the scallops with tartar sauce and lemon wedges.

scallops in cream sauce

Yield: 4 to 6 servings

2 tablespoons shortening
½ cup chopped onion
1 clove garlic, finely chopped
1 stalk celery, diced
¼ teaspoon powdered mustard

½ cup diced tart apple
1½ pounds sea scallops, cut
   in half
1 cup dry white wine or water
½ cup heavy cream

Heat shortening in cooker. Add onion, garlic, celery, mustard, and apple. Allow this to simmer for flavors to blend.

Put rack in cooker and place scallops on rack. Pour wine over all. Close cover and put pressure regulator in place. When pressure is reached and regulator jiggles, remove from heat and cool cooker under running water.

Return open cooker to a low heat. Remove the rack, lifting it out with a fork. Add heavy cream. Stir to heat; serve.

scallops in lemon butter

Yield: 4 to 6 servings

4 cups scallops
1 cup white wine
½ teaspoon salt
1 tablespoon chopped parsley
4 tablespoons butter or margarine
2 teaspoons lemon juice

Place scallops in cooker with wine, salt, and parsley. Close cover and set pressure regulator in place. When pressure is reached and regulator jiggles gently, remove cooker from heat. Cool at once under running water.

Melt butter in a saucepan and add lemon juice. Pour over the drained scallops. Serve.

scallops and ham

Yield: 6 to 8 servings

4 cups scallops
1 cup white wine
½ teaspoon salt
4 tablespoons butter or margarine
4 spring onions, finely chopped

24 mushrooms, finely sliced
2 tablespoons minced parsley
2 tablespoons flour
4 tablespoons heavy cream
1 cup minced cooked ham

Place scallops in cooker with wine and salt. Close cover and set pressure control in place. When pressure is reached and regulator jiggles gently, remove cooker from heat. Cool at once under running water.

Drain the scallops and reserve the liquid. Set both aside.

In the open cooker, melt the butter. Add spring onions, mushrooms, and parsley.

Mix the flour in ¼ cup of the reserved liquid. Add this and the remaining liquid to the cooker. Put in heavy cream, stirring constantly. *Do not boil.* Last, add the scallops and ham to the hot sauce.

Serve at once.

shrimp in beer

Yield: 4 servings

1 pound shrimp, peeled
   and cleaned
½ stalk celery, diced
1 carrot, sliced
1 small onion, sliced

1 tablespoon lemon juice
1 teaspoon salt
1 teaspoon garlic salt
1/8 teaspoon pepper
1 cup beer

Put ingredients into cooker in order given. Close cover and put pressure control in place. When pressure is reached, cook 2 minutes. Cool cooker under running water at once. Stir and serve.

steamed shrimp

Yield: 4 servings

1½ pounds shrimp
1½ cups boiling water
1 tablespoon prepared seafood seasoning

Place rack in cooker. Put shrimp on rack and pour boiling water and seafood seasoning over it. Close cover securely and place pressure control on. Cook 3 minutes after control jiggles. Cool at once under running water.

Remove shrimp from cooker and cool in cold water. When shrimp are cool enough to handle, remove shells and black line. Prepare the cooked shrimp as desired.

shrimp in beer

shrimp creole

If your shrimp and rice are prepared ahead, this is a company dish that goes together in just a few minutes.

Yield: 4 to 6 servings

2 tablespoons shortening
1 cup diced celery
1 medium onion, sliced in rings
1 teaspoon salt
1 teaspoon chili powder
1 cup tomato juice
2 teaspoons vinegar
½ teaspoon sugar
1 cup cooked shrimp
1½ cups cooked rice

Heat shortening in cooker. Tan the celery and onions in the fat. Add the rest of ingredients in order given; mix together well. Close cover securely and set pressure regulator in place. When the regulator rocks gently, cook for 3 minutes. Cool at once under running water; serve.

83

shrimp curry with raisins

Yield: 4 servings

> 2 tablespoons shortening
> ¼ cup chopped onion
> ¼ cup sliced mushrooms
> ½ teaspoon curry powder
> ½ teaspoon salt
> Dash of pepper
> 1 pound shrimp, peeled and cleaned
> 4 lemon slices
> 1 cup bouillon
> ½ cup raisins
> 3 tablespoons flour
> 1 cup milk

Heat shortening in cooker. Lightly sauté the onion and mushrooms. Add curry powder, salt, pepper, shrimp, lemon, bouillon, and raisins. Close cover and set pressure regulator in place. When regulator jiggles gently, cook for 2 minutes. Cool at once under running water.

Combine the flour and milk and add to the liquid in open pressure cooker. Over a low flame, stir constantly until the sauce thickens.

This may be served over rice if desired.

shrimp in dill sauce

Yield: 4 servings

> 1 tablespoon chopped onion
> 2 tablespoons shortening
> 1 pound shrimp, peeled and cleaned
> 1 cup white wine
> 2 tablespoons cornstarch
> ¼ cup milk
> ¾ cup milk or cream
> 1 teaspoon dillweed

Tan the onion in shortening. Add shrimp and wine. Close cover and put pressure control in place. When pressure is reached, cook for 2 minutes. Cool cooker at once. Return open cooker to a low flame.

Mix cornstarch with ¼ cup milk. Add to shrimp, and stir until thickened. Last, add remainder of milk and dillweed. Simmer for 5 minutes.

Serve at once.

shrimp scampi

Yield: 4 to 6 servings

2 tablespoons shortening (olive oil, if you have it)
1 garlic clove, minced fine
1 pound shrimp, cooked, shelled, and deveined
1 can Italian tomatoes
⅓ cup canned tomato paste
1 tablespoon chopped parsley
¼ teaspoon oregano
⅔ cup water
Grated Parmesan cheese

Heat shortening in cooker. Brown the garlic. Add shrimp, tomatoes, tomato paste, parsley, oregano, and water. Close cover and put pressure regulator in place. When pressure is reached, cook for 3 minutes. Cool cooker at once.

Serve shrimp on a bed of spaghetti. Top with Parmesan cheese.

shrimp scampi

shrimp teriyaki

This is especially good served on hot rice, which adds to the Oriental look as well as taste.

Yield: 4 servings

   1 pound shelled, deveined raw shrimp
   ½ pound Chinese pea pods
   2 tablespoons soy sauce
   3 tablespoons vinegar
   ¾ cup pineapple juice
   3 tablespoons sugar
   1 cup chicken broth

Put shrimp and pea pods in cooker.

Combine the rest of the ingredients, mixing well so that sugar dissolves. Pour the liquid into the cooker and close cover. Set pressure control in place. When pressure is reached, cook for 2 minutes. Cool at once to lower pressure under running water. Serve.

italian-style green beans

Yield: 4 servings

> 1½ pounds green beans
> ½ cup water
> ¼ cup Italian salad dressing

Remove the ends of the beans and cut into 1-inch pieces.

Place water and salad dressing in cooker and add beans. Cover the cooker and place pressure control on top. When control indicates pressure is reached, cook for 3 minutes. Cool at once. Serve.

green beans with sour cream

Yield: 4 to 6 servings

> 1½ pounds fresh green beans, cut into 1-inch pieces
> 1 teaspoon salt
> ½ cup water
> 1 cup water chestnuts
> ½ cup sour cream

Put beans, salt, and water in cooker. Close cover and put pressure control in place. When pressure is reached, cook for 3 minutes. Cool at once under running water.

Return cooker to low flame. Add water chestnuts and sour cream. Stir until hot and blended. Serve.

Picture on next page: italian-style green beans

sweet-and-sour beans

Yield: 4 to 6 servings

1 quart green beans, cut into 1-inch pieces	vinegar
1 teaspoon salt	½ cup water
2 tablespoons sugar	2 tablespoons liquid from beans
2 tablespoons lemon juice or	1 tablespoon cornstarch

Place beans, salt, sugar, lemon juice, and water in cooker. Close cover securely and put pressure regulator in place. When regulator is rocking gently and pressure reached, cook for 3 minutes. Cool at once under running water. Open cooker.

Remove 2 tablespoons of the liquid and mix this with the cornstarch. Return liquid to beans and stir until slightly thickened. Add additional salt if needed. Serve.

lima beans in tomato sauce

Yield: 4 to 6 servings

2 packages frozen baby lima beans	1 can tomato soup
2 or 3 tomatoes, diced	2 tablespoons brown sugar
	½ cup water

Defrost frozen lima beans for ½ hour or until the block can be separated. Put lima beans in cooker. Add rest of ingredients in order given. Close cover and put pressure control in place. When pressure is reached, cook for 2 minutes. Cool at once under running water.

Stir the vegetables gently. Serve.

beets in sour cream

Yield: 4 servings

3 cups beets, diced or sliced	½ cup sour cream
¾ cup water	1 tablespoon horseradish
	1 tablespoon chopped chives

Place beets in cooker with water. Close cover of cooker and set pressure regulator in place. When pressure is reached, cook for 6 minutes. Cool at once. When pressure is reduced, drain the beets and allow to cool.

Mix sour cream, horseradish, and chives. Pour over the chilled beets; mix gently. Serve.

If you prefer hot beets in a hot sauce, warm the sour cream, horseradish, and chives over a double boiler. Pour over hot beets.

special sliced beets

Some people feel there is no way to make beets special. Hopefully, they will be in for a surprise with this recipe. These are delicious served hot and are also very good in a chilled salad.

Yield: 4 to 6 servings

> **3 cups sliced beets**
> **¼ cup sugar**
> **½ teaspoon salt**
> **¾ cup orange juice**

Put beets into cooker.

Dissolve sugar and salt in orange juice; pour over beets. Close cooker cover securely; put pressure control in place. When pressure is reached, cook for 6 minutes. Cool cooker at once under running water.

broccoli in cream sauce

Yield: 4 to 6 servings

> **2 pounds broccoli (about 3 cups)**
> **1 10-ounce can cream of celery soup**
> **1 cup water**
> **½ teaspoon salt**

Wash broccoli. Cut stems in 1-inch pieces, leaving florets a little longer. Use all the broccoli. Put broccoli in cooker.

Mix undiluted soup with water and add salt. Pour over the broccoli. Close cover on cooker. Set pressure control in place. When pressure is reached, cook 3 minutes. Cool cooker at once under running water. Serve.

brussels sprouts and new potatoes

Yield: 4 to 6 servings

> **1½ pounds Brussels sprouts**
> **1 cup new potatoes, peeled and diced**
> **½ cup beef or chicken broth**
> **1½ tablespoons bread crumbs**
> **1½ tablespoons butter**

Wash and clean the vegetables. Put in cooker with liquid. Close cover of cooker and put pressure control in place. When pressure is reached, cook for 5 minutes. Cool at once under faucet.

Thoroughly mix the bread crumbs and melted butter. Spoon over the drained hot vegetables. Serve.

cabbage in mushroom sauce

Yield: 4 servings

3 cups shredded cabbage
½ teaspoon salt
1 10-ounce can cream of mushroom soup
1 cup water
½ cup grated cheese (your choice cheddar or Parmesan)

Wash and shred cabbage coarsely. Place cabbage in cooker and sprinkle with salt.

Mix mushroom soup and water together until blended, then pour over the cabbage. Close cover and set pressure control in place. When pressure is reached, cook for 3 minutes. Reduce pressure at once under faucet. Open cooker and stir cabbage.

Sprinkle with grated cheese, and serve.

cabbage in meat essence

The bouillon or beef broth in which you cook this cabbage adds special flavor to the common leafy vegetable. Cabbage-haters may even find it tasty this way.

Yield: 4 to 6 servings

1 medium head cabbage, shredded
1 teaspoon lemon-pepper seasoning
½ cup beef broth

Put shredded cabbage, seasoning, and beef broth into cooker. Close cover securely; put pressure control in place. When pressure is reached, cook for 3 minutes with control rocking gently. Cool at once under running water. Serve.

cabbage and rice

Yield: 4 to 6 servings

½ cup finely chopped onion
3 tablespoons shortening
3 cups coarsely shredded cabbage

1 green pepper, diced
1 cup rice
2 cups canned tomatoes
½ cup beef broth

In cooker, brown onions lightly in shortening. Add cabbage, green pepper, rice, tomatoes, and beef broth. Close cover of cooker and set pressure control in place. When pressure control is rocking gently, cook for 1 minute. Allow pressure to drop naturally.

Be sure to mix vegetables well just before serving.

cabbage with apples

Yield: 4 to 6 servings

1½ pounds cabbage,
    shredded
3 apples, peeled and diced
½ teaspoon salt
½ teaspoon sugar
2 tablespoons lemon juice
¼ cup water
1 tablespoon cornstarch
2 tablespoons water
½ cup sour cream
1 teaspoon dill leaves
1 teaspoon chopped parsley

Place cabbage, apples, salt, sugar, lemon juice, and ¼ cup water in cooker. Close cover and put pressure regulator in place. When pressure is reached, cook for 3 minutes. Cool at once under running water. Open cooker and return to a low flame.

Mix cornstarch with 2 tablespoons water and add to cooker. Stir until slightly thickened or until mixture comes to a boil. Add sour cream, dill, and parsley. Serve.

chinese cabbage with mushrooms

Yield: 4 to 6 servings

1 medium head Chinese cabbage,
    washed and cut into
    1½-inch pieces
½ pound fresh mushrooms, diced
1 teaspoon salt
½ cup water
4 tablespoons melted butter

Place cabbage, mushrooms, salt, and water in cooker. Close cover and set pressure control in place. When pressure is reached and control jiggles gently, cook for 3 minutes. Cool cooker at once under running water.

Put vegetables in serving dish and pour melted butter on top.

sweet-and-sour red cabbage

Yield: 4 to 6 servings

2 tablespoons shortening or
   bacon drippings
4 to 5 cups shredded red
   cabbage
1 medium onion, sliced
1 cup sliced apples

½ cup seedless raisins
1 teaspoon salt
Dash of pepper
2 tablespoons brown sugar
¼ cup vinegar
¼ cup red wine

Heat shortening in cooker. Add rest of ingredients in the order given. Close cover and set pressure control in place. When pressure is reached and control jiggles, cook 4 minutes. Reduce pressure at once under running water. Serve.

sweet-and-sour red cabbage

carrots, raisins, and pineapple

This sweet vegetable may make a carrot-lover of the worst of them.

Yield: 4 to 6 servings

3 cups sliced carrots
1 cup pineapple juice
½ cup raisins
1 20-ounce can pineapple chunks,
    drained

1 tablespoon cornstarch
¼ teaspoon salt
¼ cup water
1 tablespoon butter or
    margarine

Put carrots, pineapple juice, and raisins in cooker. Close cover securely and set pressure regulator in place. When pressure is reached, cook for 2 to 3 minutes. Reduce pressure at once. With cooker open and over a very low flame, add pineapple chunks.

Mix cornstarch, salt, and water together and add to carrots. Stir until slightly thickened, being careful not to break up carrots. Add butter. Serve.

celery and almonds

Yield: 4 to 6 servings

2 or 3 cups celery, cut into
    2-inch strips
1 small onion, chopped fine
1 teaspoon salt
½ cup chicken broth
½ cup slivered almonds

Put celery, onion, salt, and chicken broth in cooker. Close cover and put pressure control in place. When pressure is reached, cook 3 minutes. Cool cooker at once under running water.

Add almonds to celery; simmer together for 1 or 2 minutes more. Serve.

scalloped corn

Yield: 4 to 6 servings

2 cups uncooked corn, cut off the cob
1 cup diced green pepper
¼ cup chopped olives
½ cup water

Put corn, green pepper, and olives into cooker; pour water over them. (No salt in this one—the olives will supply that.) Close cover securely; put pressure control in place. When pressure is reached and control rocks gently, cook for 3 minutes. Reduce pressure at once under running water.

Stir to blend the vegetables. **Serve at once.**

ratatouille I

If you have a prolific vegetable garden, ratatouille is for you. When produce is plentiful, this is an ideal dish, served hot or cold.

Yield: 4 to 6 servings

2 cups eggplant, diced
   and peeled
1 cup sliced onions
2 green peppers, cut into strips
2 cups diced zucchini

2 medium-size tomatoes,
   quartered
2 teaspoons salt
½ teaspoon oregano
2 tablespoons water

Place all of your prepared vegetables in the cooker. Sprinkle with salt and oregano. Add water. Close the cover and put the pressure control in place. When pressure is reached, allow to cook for 2 to 3 minutes. Cool at once under running water. Serve.

95

ratatouille II

Yield: 4 to 6 servings

2 cups diced, peeled eggplant
1 cup sliced onions
2 green peppers, cut in strips
1 cup diced zucchini
1 cup diced summer squash

2 medium-size tomatoes,
    quartered
2 teaspoons salt
½ teaspoon garlic salt
2 tablespoons water

Prepare vegetables in the order given and put into the cooker. Add salt, garlic salt, and water. Close cover securely and put pressure regulator in place. When pressure is reached, allow to cook for 2 to 3 minutes. Cool at once under running water. Serve.

If you prefer the taste of celery, 1 cup of diced celery is a happy substitute for one of the vegetables above.

easy creamed onions

Yield: 4 to 6 servings

1 pound small onions, peeled
½ teaspoon salt
½ teaspoon cloves
1 teaspoon sugar
½ cup water
1 can cream of mushroom soup
1 cup seasoned croutons

Put onions, salt, cloves, sugar, and water into cooker. Close cover and put pressure control in place. When pressure is reached, cook for 5 minutes. Cool cooker at once. Open cooker and put on a low flame.

Add the cream of mushroom soup and stir to mix. Last, put in the croutons. Give one last stir, and serve.

onions and dates

This is delicious as a vegetable or as a sweet-and-sour garnish for meat.

Yield: 4 servings

4 large onions, cut into
    ¼-inch rings
1 teaspoon shortening

1 teaspoon salt
¼ to ½ cup chopped dates
½ cup red wine

Put onions in cooker. Add rest of ingredients in order given. Put cover on cooker and set pressure regulator in place. When pressure is reached, cook for 4 minutes. Cool at once. Serve.

onions in raisin sauce

Yield: 4 servings

4 large onions, cut into ¼-inch rings
1 teaspoon shortening
1 tablespoon wine vinegar
1 teaspoon salt
1 teaspoon oregano (optional)
¼ cup raisins
½ cup water

Place ingredients in cooker in order given. Close cover and put pressure control in place. When control indicates pressure is reached, cook for 4 minutes. Cool at once under running water. Serve.

creamed peas and carrots

Yield: 4 to 6 servings

1½ cups diced carrots
2 cups shelled peas
1 10-ounce can cream of mushroom soup
½ cup water
½ teaspoon salt

Put peas and carrots together in the cooker.
Mix the soup and water. Pour over the vegetables. Add salt. Close cooker and set pressure regulator in place. When pressure is reached, cook for 2 minutes. Cool at once under running water. Serve.

dill peas and cucumbers

Yield: 4 servings

1 cup shelled peas
1 cup diced cucumber, with skin left on
½ cup water
1 teaspoon dillseed

Put shelled peas and cucumber into cooker. Add water and dillseed. Cover and set pressure control on. When pressure is reached, cook for 1 minute. Cool instantly under faucet.
Drain, and serve with melted butter, if desired.

sweet potatoes and apples

Yield: 4 to 6 servings

6 sweet potatoes, peeled and sliced
2 cups apples, peeled and sliced
1 cup thin maple syrup
2 tablespoons melted butter or margarine
2 teaspoons salt
½ cup water

Place sweet potatoes and apples in cooker in alternate layers, ending with sweet potatoes on top.

Combine the remaining ingredients and pour over potatoes and apples. Close cover of cooker and set pressure control in place. When pressure is reached, cook for 5 minutes. Cool at once under running water. Serve.

sliced potatoes and onions

Yield: 4 to 6 servings

4 large potatoes, peeled and sliced
2 tablespoons shortening
2 medium onions, cut in rings
1 teaspoon salt
½ cup water
Parmesan cheese

Peel and slice potatoes; set aside in cold water to keep from turning dark.

Heat shortening in cooker; tan the onions. Add potatoes, salt, and water. Close cover of cooker securely; put pressure control in place. When pressure is reached, cook for 3 minutes. Cool at once under running water.

Place potatoes in serving dish and sprinkle with Parmesan cheese. The heat of the potatoes will melt the cheese so that all flavors blend.

potatoes supreme

These potatoes are delicious around a roast or with chops.

Yield: 4 to 6 servings

4 large potatoes, peeled and quartered
2 tablespoons shortening
1 medium onion, chopped fine
1 cup beef broth

Peel and quarter potatoes. Set aside in cold water so they do not darken.

Heat shortening in cooker; lightly tan the onion. Onion should be transparent, not browned. Add drained potatoes and beef broth. Close cover of cooker; put pressure control in place. When pressure is reached, cook for 4 minutes. Cool at once under running water.

sweet potatoes and pineapple

Yield: 4 to 6 servings

> 4 sweet potatoes, peeled
> and quartered
> 1 can pineapple chunks, drained
> ¼ cup brown sugar
> 1 teaspoon salt
> 1 cup pineapple juice
> 2 tablespoons butter or
> margarine

Place ingredients in the pressure cooker in order given. Close cover and set pressure control in place. When pressure is reached, cook for 8 minutes. Cool at once under running water.

If desired, remove potatoes and pineapple chunks to serving bowl, thicken syrup, and pour over the vegetables.

radishes

40-minute potato salad

Yield: 6 to 8 servings

3 pounds potatoes
1 cup water
2 tablespoons salad oil
2½ tablespoons vinegar
1 tablespoon chopped parsley
1 small onion, chopped fine
¼ cup chopped green pepper
¾ cup diced celery
1 teaspoon salt
1 teaspoon dillseed
¾ cup mayonnaise

Wash and prepare the potatoes, cutting very large ones in half.

Place water in the cooker. Add the rack and then the potatoes. Close cover securely and place the pressure regulator on the cooker. When regulator rocks slowly, cook for 10 minutes.

While the potatoes are cooking, assemble and prepare the rest of the ingredients.

When cooking time is finished, cool the cooker at once under running water. Remove and dice the potatoes. Add the remaining ingredients to the diced potatoes in the order given, mixing carefully with a rubber spatula.

Put the potato salad in a bowl and chill until time to eat.

creamed radishes

Radishes are a neglected vegetable but very delicious. Try this on your family. Good and easy.

Yield: 4 to 6 servings

1 pound young radishes
2 teaspoons salt
½ cup water
1 can cream of celery soup

Remove stems and roots of radishes. Leave the skin on. Cut any large radishes in half.

Put radishes, salt, and water in the pressure cooker. Close cover and set pressure regulator in place. When pressure is reached, cook for 2 minutes. Cool cooker at once and remove cover.

Pour undiluted cream of celery soup over the radishes and simmer until blended and hot.

Serve at once.

40-minute potato salad

browned white rice

Yield: 4 to 6 servings

> 2 medium onions, chopped fine
> 1 tablespoon shortening
> 1 green pepper, chopped
> 1 cup rice
> 2 cups beef broth

Tan onions lightly in shortening. Add green pepper, rice, and beef broth. Close cooker cover securely and put pressure control in place. When pressure is reached and control jiggles gently, remove cooker from heat. Allow to cool naturally.

Stir rice gently with a fork to fluff, and serve.

rice with chicken broth

Yield: 4 to 6 servings

> 2 cups chicken broth
> 1 cup white rice
> 1 onion, finely minced
> ½ teaspoon saffron (optional)
> ¼ cup butter

Place chicken broth in cooker and bring to a boil. Add the rice and onion. Close cover on cooker and place pressure control on it. When pressure is reached and control rocking gently, remove cooker from heat. Allow to cool naturally.

After opening cooker, add saffron and butter to rice. Serve at once.

fluffy white rice

Yield: 4 to 6 servings

> 2 cups water
> ½ teaspoon salt
> 1 cup white rice
> 2 teaspoons lemon juice

Put water into cooker and bring to a rolling boil. Add salt, rice, and lemon juice. Close cover and set pressure regulator in place. When regulator is rocking gently, remove rice from heat and set aside to allow pressure to drop naturally.

Serve at once, fluffing rice with a fork if necessary.

Picture on opposite page: fluffy white rice

fried rice

Yield: 4 to 6 servings

2 tablespoons shortening
1 onion, finely diced
1 cup white rice
2 cups water
1 tablespoon soy sauce
½ teaspoon sugar

Dash of pepper
1 2-ounce can sliced pimientos,
    drained
2 tablespoons cooking sherry
2 whole tomatoes, peeled, diced,
    and seeded

Heat shortening in cooker. Brown onion and rice. Add the rest of the ingredients and close cover of cooker securely. Place pressure control on the top. Allow this to cook until the pressure control rocks gently. Remove cooker from heat and allow pressure to drop naturally.

If desired, place the cooked rice in a baking pan and brown under the broiler for 5 minutes. Serve at once.

rice with gruyere cheese

Yield: 4 to 6 servings

2 tablespoons shortening
1 medium onion, chopped
1 cup rice
½ cup dry white wine
1½ cups chicken broth
½ cup grated Gruyere cheese

Heat shortening and lightly tan onion. Add rice, wine, and chicken broth. Close cover and put pressure regulator in place. When the regulator is rocking gently and pressure is reached, remove from heat. Allow cooker to cool normally. When pressure is fully reduced, open cooker.

Fold in the cheese until it has blended. It will melt very quickly. Serve at once.

oriental rice

Yield: 4 to 6 servings

1 tablespoon butter or margarine
1 cup white rice
½ cup white wine
1½ cups chicken broth

½ teaspoon salt
¼ teaspoon pepper
1 cup sliced mushrooms
1 tablespoon chopped parsley

Place all ingredients in the pressure cooker in the order given. Cover the cooker and put pressure control in place. When pressure is reached, remove cooker from heat and allow pressure to drop of its own accord.

Stir the hot rice gently with a fork to fluff it. Serve at once.

fried rice

lemon rice

Yield: 4 to 6 servings

2 tablespoons shortening
1 cup diced celery
1 cup green onions with tops
1 cup rice
1 tablespoon grated lemon rind
    (optional)

1 teaspoon salt
¼ teaspoon pepper
1 cup water plus
    2 tablespoons lemon juice

Heat shortening in cooker. Lightly tan celery and onions. Add rice, lemon rind, salt, pepper, and water mixture. Close cover of cooker and put pressure control in place. When pressure is reached, remove cooker from the flame. Allow to cool normally.

When cool, open cooker and stir rice with a fork to fluff. Serve.

105

summer rice

This dish has as many variations as there are fresh vegetables and is a boon to the gardener who has a super harvest.

Yield: 4 to 6 servings

2 medium onions, cut in quarters
1 large zucchini, sliced in rings
1 cup yellow corn
1 green pepper, cut into
    1-inch pieces
2 large tomatoes, quartered

8 radishes, cut in half
2 cups rice
1 teaspoon salt
¼ teaspoon pepper
1 teaspoon dillweed or fresh dill
½ cup water

Place vegetables in cooker in order given. Add seasonings and water and close cover securely. Put pressure control in place. When pressure is reached, cook for 3 minutes. Cool at once.

Stir vegetables, and serve.

zesty rice

Yield: 4 to 6 servings

1 10½-ounce can beef broth
Enough water to make 2 cups of liquid
1 cup white rice
1 teaspoon oregano
½ teaspoon salt

Place contents of can of broth plus enough water to make 2 cups liquid in the cooker. Bring this to a boil. Add rice, oregano, and salt. Close cover on cooker. Put pressure control in place. When pressure is reached, remove rice from heat. Allow to cool naturally. Serve.

pineapple sauerkraut

Delicious with any pork dish.

Yield: 4 to 6 servings

2 pounds sauerkraut, drained
2½ cups pineapple chunks
½ cup pineapple juice

Place ingredients in cooker in order given. Close cover and put pressure control in place. When pressure is reached, cook for 5 minutes. Cool at once, and serve.

Picture on opposite page: summer rice

thanksgiving sauerkraut

This is almost a meal in itself.

Yield: 4 to 6 servings

2 tablespoons shortening
½ pound stew meat, cut into 1-inch cubes
½ cup sliced onion
1 quart sauerkraut
2 tablespoons brown sugar
1 cup canned tomatoes with juice

Heat shortening in cooker; brown the stew meat and onion. Add remaining ingredients as listed, dissolving sugar in tomatoes. Close cover of cooker securely; put pressure control in place. When pressure is reached, cook for 12 minutes. Allow cooker to cool normally. When cooker has been uncovered, stir sauerkraut gently.

Serve sauerkraut, with the meat, in a serving bowl.

spinach supreme

Yield: 4 to 6 servings

2 packages frozen chopped spinach,
    thawed for ½ hour before cooking
1 clove garlic, minced
1 teaspoon salt
½ cup water
6 or more anchovies, chopped

Break up the frozen spinach into small blocks. Place spinach, garlic, salt, and water in cooker. Close cover and put pressure regulator in place. When pressure is reached, cook 1 minute. Cool at once under running water.

Add chopped anchovies to spinach and stir to blend flavors. Serve hot.

summer squash and onions

Yield: 4 to 6 servings

3 cups diced summer squash
2 cups onion rings
1 teaspoon salt
½ teaspoon pepper
½ cup tomato juice

Prepare vegetables as directed; put them into pressure cooker. Add salt and pepper; stir gently to mix. Pour tomato juice over. Close cover of cooker; put pressure regulator in place. When pressure is reached and regulator rocking gently, cook for 3 minutes. Cool at once under running water.

Put vegetables into serving bowl; serve at once.

acorn squash

This should be called Autumn Delight because it is certainly a time of harvest when acorn squash are plentiful. You need a sharp knife to cut them, but they are worth the trouble.

Yield: 2 servings per whole squash

1 acorn squash
2 tablespoons honey
Dash of nutmeg
¾ cup water

Wash and halve squash. Remove seeds. Put 1 tablespoon honey in each half. Sprinkle each half with nutmeg.

Place water in cooker and put rack above it. Put squash on rack. Close cover; put pressure control in place. When pressure is reached and control jiggles gently, cook for 7 minutes. Cool at once under running water. Serve.

spinach supreme

109

green-bean succotash

Yield: 4 to 6 servings

> **2 cups uncooked corn off the cob**
> **2 cups green beans, cut into 1-inch pieces**
> **1 teaspoon salt**
> **½ cup water**

Combine all ingredients in cooker in order given. Close cover securely; place pressure control on air vent. When control jiggles gently and pressure is reached, cook for 3 minutes. Cool cooker at once.

Dot the succotash with butter, and serve it piping hot.

summer succotash

Yield: 4 to 6 servings

> **2 cups uncooked fresh corn off the cob**
> **2 cups baby lima beans**
> **½ cup pineapple juice**
> **½ teaspoon salt**

Put corn, lima beans, and pineapple juice in cooker together. Sprinkle with salt. Close cover securely; set pressure regulator in place. When pressure is reached, cook for 2 minutes. Cool cooker at once under running water.

Stir the vegetables gently, and put them into a serving dish. Dot with butter if you wish.

tomatoes and okra

Yield: 4 to 6 servings

> **2 tablespoons shortening**
> **½ cup finely chopped onion**
> **2 cups sliced okra**
> **2 cups fresh tomatoes**
> **1 teaspoon salt**
> **½ teaspoon paprika**
> **2 teaspoons brown sugar**
> **¼ cup water**

Heat shortening in cooker; tan the onion. Add okra and tomatoes.

Dissolve salt, paprika, and brown sugar in water; pour over vegetables. Close cover of cooker securely; put pressure regulator in place. When pressure is reached, cook for 3 minutes. Cool cooker at once under running water.

Stir the vegetables, and serve them hot.

green tomatoes

Instead of waiting for a bumper crop of green tomatoes to ripen, try some of them this way. They go well with corn on the cob.

Yield: 4 to 6 servings

> **4 to 6 green tomatoes, quartered**
> **½ cup sugar**
> **½ cup water**

Place tomatoes, sugar, and water in cooker. Close cover and put pressure control in place. When control jiggles gently, remove from heat and cool cooker at once under running water.

Stir and serve the tomatoes.

stewed green tomatoes

Yield: 4 to 6 servings

> **3 cups sliced green tomatoes**
> **2 tablespoons shortening**
> **2 tablespoons minced onion**
> **¾ teaspoon salt**
> **¼ teaspoon paprika**
> **½ teaspoon curry powder (optional)**
> **¼ cup water**

Slice tomatoes; set aside.

Melt shortening in cooker; brown the onions. Add sliced tomatoes and rest of ingredients in order given, ending with water. Close cover securely; put pressure control in place. When pressure is reached, cook for 2 minutes. Cool cooker at once.

Serve the tomatoes hot.

turnips in tomato sauce

Yield: 4 to 6 servings

> **4 to 6 medium turnips, peeled and diced**
> **1 teaspoon salt**
> **1 teaspoon sugar**
> **½ cup water**
> **1 can condensed tomato soup**

Put turnips, salt, sugar, and water into cooker. Close cover and put pressure control in place. When pressure is reached, cook for 3 minutes. Cool cooker at once under running water. Open cooker and return to a low flame.

Add the condensed tomato soup and simmer for 3 minutes more or until the flavors are well-blended and the turnips are hot. Serve.

zucchini, corn, and tomatoes

Yield: 4 to 6 servings

> 2 pounds zucchini, diced or cut into wheels
> 2 or 3 tomatoes, quartered
> 1 cup corn off the cob
> 1 teaspoon salt
> 1 teaspoon sugar
> ½ cup water
> 2 tablespoons butter or margarine

Place ingredients into pressure cooker in order given. Close cover and set pressure control in place. When control jiggles gently, cook for 3 minutes. Cool cooker at once under running water.

Put in serving dish and dot with butter. Serve.

One-Pot Dinners

beef goulash a la ginny

Ginny is a friend to whom time and her pressure cooker are both important. She makes this Goulash after a busy day, in less than 1 hour.

Yield: 4 to 6 servings

2 tablespoons shortening
2 pounds stew meat, cubed into
    1-inch pieces
1 large onion, sliced
1 10½-ounce can tomato soup plus
    enough water to make
    1 cup liquid

1 cup diced potatoes
1 cup diced carrots
1 cup cut green beans
1 cup sliced mushrooms
    (optional)
2 teaspoons salt

Heat shortening in cooker. Brown the meat and sliced onions together. Add the liquid, vegetables, and salt. Close cover securely and set pressure regulator in place. When pressure is reached, cook for 10 minutes. Allow to cool naturally.

Ginny says this stew is even better if you allow it to refrigerate overnight and serve it hot the next evening.

autumn harvest (beef and eggplant)

This recipe calls for eggplant. Use any of your abundant garden produce in its place.

Yield: 4 to 6 servings

2 pounds beef, cut into
    1-inch cubes
1 onion, chopped
1 garlic clove, crushed
2 tablespoons shortening
3 tomatoes, chopped

1 eggplant, peeled and cubed
1 teaspoon paprika
½ teaspoon oregano
1 teaspoon salt
Dash of pepper
Parsley for garnish

Brown meat, onion, and garlic in shortening. Add rest of ingredients (except parsley) in order given. Close cooker and put pressure control in place. When pressure is reached, cook for 12 minutes. Cool at once.

Garnish with parsley, if desired, and serve.

Picture on next pages: beef goulash a la ginny

petite marmite

Yield: 6 servings

 2 tablespoons shortening
 2 pounds beef in 1 piece
 1 pound chicken wings
 1 onion stuck with 3 cloves
 3 medium-size leeks, white parts only
 3 small ribs celery
 2 cups diced white turnips
 2 carrots, diced
 1 cup diced potatoes
 1 bay leaf
 1 teaspoon salt
 6 peppercorns
 4 cups beef broth

Heat shortening in cooker and brown meat on all sides. Put rest of ingredients in cooker in order given. Close cover and put pressure control in place. When pressure is reached and control jiggles, cook for 30 minutes. Allow cooker to cool naturally. When pressure is fully reduced, open cooker and remove meat and chicken wings.

Slice the meat and put a slice in each soup bowl, with vegetables and broth over it. Serve.

one-pot meat-loaf dinner

Yield: 4 servings

 1 pound ground beef
 1 teaspoon salt
 Dash of pepper
 1 egg, slightly beaten
 1 medium onion, chopped
 ¼ cup corn-flake crumbs
 1 tablespoon shortening
 1 8-ounce can tomato sauce
 ½ cup water
 4 whole potatoes, peeled
 4 whole carrots

Mix together the ground beef, salt, pepper, beaten egg, onion, and corn-flake crumbs. Shape into a loaf and wrap in foil. Refrigerate for several hours (or overnight) to prevent loaf from falling apart.

Melt shortening in cooker and brown meat loaf on all sides. Remove.

Put tomato sauce and water into cooker. Add rack and arrange the meat loaf and vegetables on the rack. Close cover; put pressure control in place. When pressure is reached, cook for 12 to 15 minutes. Cool cooker normally for 5 minutes, then cool it under the faucet. Serve.

minced-beef stew

This stew is different, but be ready for compliments.

Yield: 4 to 6 servings

2 tablespoons shortening
1 pound beef, minced preferred, but ground twice will do
2 medium onions, sliced
1 tomato, diced
2 cups diced potatoes
1 teaspoon salt
¼ teaspoon pepper
½ cup beef broth
2 pears, peeled and sliced
2 peaches, peeled and sliced
4 plums, peeled and sliced
¼ cup seedless raisins

Heat shortening in cooker. Brown meat and onions together. Add tomato, potatoes, salt, pepper, and beef broth. Close cover securely and put pressure control in place. When pressure is reached, cook for 5 minutes. Cool cooker at once under running water.

Return open cooker to flame. Add the fruit in the order given. Stir and cook for 3 minutes more. Serve.

minced-beef stew

hamburger vegetable stew

Although this is a complete meal, you might want to add a salad. With a loaf of homemade bread, it is a party.

Yield: 4 to 6 servings

2 tablespoons shortening
½ to l pound ground beef
1 cup canned tomatoes
½ cup diced carrots
½ cup diced celery
1 onion, chopped, or ½ cup spring onions
2 teaspoons salt
¼ cup rice
Dash of pepper
1½ cups water
1 cup diced potatoes

Heat shortening in cooker. Brown the meat. Add the tomatoes, carrots, celery, onion, salt, rice, pepper, and water. Last, add the potatoes. Close the cooker and place the pressure regulator in position. When pressure is reached and regulator is gently rocking, cook for 5 minutes. Allow to cool naturally. Serve.

sweet meat stew

Yield: 4 to 6 servings

1½ pounds lean ground beef
¾ cup bread crumbs
2 eggs
1 teaspoon oregano
1 teaspoon salt
¼ teaspoon pepper
2 tablespoons shortening
2 cups drained pineapple cubes
1 green pepper, chopped
2 cups chopped canned peaches
1 cup rice
1 cup water

Mix meat, bread crumbs, eggs, oregano, salt, and pepper in a bowl. Form mixture into meatballs.

Heat shortening in cooker. Brown meatballs. Add the rest of the ingredients. Close cover and put pressure control in place. When pressure is reached, cook for 8 minutes. Cool cooker at once, and serve.

tasty lamb stew

Yield: 4 to 6 servings

> 2 pounds lamb, cut into 1-inch cubes
> 2 tablespoons shortening
> 1 onion, sliced
> 2 carrots, sliced
> ½ teaspoon oregano
> ½ teaspoon garlic salt
> 1 teaspoon salt
> Dash of pepper
> 1 cup dry red wine
> 1 10-ounce package frozen peas
> ¼ pound sliced mushrooms

Brown lamb cubes in shortening. Add onion, carrots, seasonings, and wine. Close cover and put pressure regulator in place. When pressure is reached, cook for 10 minutes. Cool cooker at once under running water. Return open cooker to low flame.

Add peas and mushrooms; simmer for 5 minutes more.

Thicken gravy slightly, if desired, and serve.

lamb-chop ragout

Your meat and vegetables are all here. All you need to add is a salad.

Yield: 6 servings

> 6 lamb chops, shoulder cut
> ¼ cup flour
> Salt and pepper to taste
> 2 tablespoons shortening
> 1 cup strong chicken broth
> 2 teaspoons steak or Worcestershire sauce
> 1 cup sliced onions
> 6 small whole carrots
> 6 medium potatoes, sliced

Dredge lamb chops in flour and salt and pepper.

Heat shortening in cooker and brown chops on both sides. Add rest of ingredients in order given. Close cover securely and set pressure control in place. When pressure is reached, cook for 8 minutes. Allow pressure to drop naturally.

Dish and serve ragout.

pork and pineapple curry

Yield: 4 to 6 servings

    1 tablespoon shortening
    1 clove garlic, minced fine
    1 medium onion, chopped
    1 pound pork, cut into l-inch pieces
    l cup rice
    2 tablespoons soy sauce
    1 teaspoon ground ginger
    ½ teaspoon saffron
    2 ounces blanched almonds
    2 cups drained pineapple chunks
    1 cup pineapple juice

Heat shortening in cooker and brown garlic and onions, adding and mixing in the pork. Add rest of ingredients. Close cover and put pressure control in place. When pressure is reached, cook for 10 minutes. Cool cooker at once under running water. Serve.

pork stew

Yield: 4 to 6 servings

    2 pounds lean pork, cut into 3- by l-inch strips
    2 tablespoons shortening
    1 tablespoon paprika
    1 large onion, chopped
    2 whole carrots, cut in 3-inch strips
    1 whole green pepper, cut in strips
    2 medium tomatoes, chopped
    1 cup sliced fresh mushrooms
    1 teaspoon salt
    ¼ teaspoon pepper
    ¾ cup water
    1 tablespoon cornstarch
    1 cup sour cream

Brown pork strips in heated shortening. Add paprika and onion; mix well. Put in carrots, green pepper, tomatoes, mushrooms, salt, pepper, and ½ cup water. Close cover and put pressure control in place. When pressure is reached, cook for 10 minutes. Let pressure drop of its own accord.

Mix cornstarch with ¼ cup water and add to open cooker. Stir until slightly thickened. Keep stirring as you add the sour cream.

When all is hot, serve the stew with buttered noodles.

wonderful western dinner

This popular western dish will be popular in your house, too.

Yield: 4 to 6 servings

½ pound link pork sausage
2 to 3 pounds chicken, cut into serving pieces
1 onion, minced
2 cups canned tomatoes with juice
18 stuffed green olives
¼ cup olive juice
1 cup rice
1 cup water
1 package frozen peas (thawed)

Brown sausage in cooker and pour off most of excess fat. Leave about 2 table-spoons fat in cooker. Set sausage aside.

Brown the chicken. Add onion, tomatoes, olives and juice, rice, water, and sausage. Close cover and put pressure control in place. When pressure is reached, cook for 15 minutes. Allow pressure to drop naturally.

Return open cooker to low flame. Add peas and simmer for 3 minutes, stirring gently. Serve.

veal and spinach delight

Yield: 6 servings

2 pounds veal, cut into 1-inch cubes
2 tablespoons shortening
1 large onion, sliced
½ cup minced green onions with tops
1 garlic clove, crushed fine
⅓ cup tomato paste
2 pounds fresh spinach, cleaned and cut up
1 teaspoon salt
Dash of pepper
½ cup water
1 cup plain yogurt
1 tablespoon dillweed

Brown veal in shortening. Add onion, green onions, garlic, tomato paste, spinach, salt, pepper, and water. Close cover and put pressure control in place. When pressure is reached, cook for 15 minutes. Cool at once under running water. Return open cooker to a low flame.

Add the yogurt and dill. Simmer until yogurt is hot and blended in.
Serve at once.

veal stew

Yield: 4 servings

3 tablespoons shortening
2 pounds veal, cut into
   2-inch cubes
1 teaspoon salt
Dash of pepper

1½ cups cooking wine
1 tablespoon sugar (optional)
4 medium potatoes
4 medium whole carrots
4 medium onions

Heat cooker and add shortening. Brown veal cubes in hot fat. Add salt, pepper, wine, and sugar. Close cover securely and put pressure control in place. When pressure is reached and control jiggles, cook for 8 minutes.

While meat is cooking, scrub potatoes and carrots. Remove skin from onions.

After 8 minutes, allow cooker to cool for 5 minutes. Then place cooker under faucet to reduce all pressure. Open cooker and put vegetables on top of veal. Again, close cover and put control in place. When pressure is reached, cook for 8 minutes more. Reduce pressure at once under running water.

Add a salad and your meal is complete.

bouillabaisse

Yield: 6 servings

2 tablespoons shortening
2 onions, chopped
1 clove garlic, minced
3 pounds mixed fish, cleaned,
   cut into chunks
4 medium potatoes,
   diced

1 bay leaf
1 teaspoon thyme
½ teaspoon rosemary
2 parsley sprigs
1 teaspoon salt
½ teaspoon pepper
4 cups water

Heat shortening in cooker. Saute the onions and garlic. Add the rest of ingredients and close cover of cooker securely. Put pressure regulator in place. When pressure is reached, cook for 3 minutes. Cool cooker at once.

Ladle the broth into soup bowls, with portions of fish and potatoes in each. Complete dinner with French bread and a salad.

bouillabaisse

stuffed eggplant

Yield: 2 servings, but worth doubling to serve 4.

1 medium eggplant	1 teaspoon dill leaves
1 cup finely chopped	1 egg
leftover meat	½ teaspoon salt
½ cup cooked rice	¼ teaspoon pepper
1 medium onion, chopped	½ cup water

sauce

	1 tablespoon tomato paste
1 tablespoon cornstarch	½ teaspoon sugar
¼ cup beef broth	Parsley for garnish

Cut eggplant lengthwise and scoop out center seeds.

Mix meat, rice, onion, dill, egg, salt, and pepper in a bowl. Fill hollowed out eggplant with this stuffing.

Put water in cooker, add rack, and place stuffed eggplants on rack. Close cover and put pressure control in place. When pressure is reached, cook for 2 to 3 minutes. Cool cooker at once. Put eggplants on a baking dish.

Dissolve cornstarch in beef broth and put in a saucepan. Add tomato paste and sugar and blend until sauce is slightly thickened. Pour over the eggplant. Place under the broiler for 2 minutes more.

Sprinkle with parsley, and serve. A tossed salad completes the meal.

apple chicken and rice

Yield: 4 to 6 servings

2 to 3 pounds chicken, cut into serving pieces
Salt and pepper
2 tablespoons shortening
1 large onion, chopped
1 apple, cored and quartered
1 cup rice
1½ cups apple juice
¼ cup heavy cream
Parsley for garnish

Season the chicken pieces liberally with salt and pepper.

Heat the shortening in cooker. Brown the onion and chicken. Add apple, rice, and apple juice. Close cover. Put pressure regulator in place. When pressure is reached, cook 15 minutes. Allow the cooker to cool normally.

Return open cooker to a low heat and add the cream. Stir gently to mix and heat.

Garnish with parsley, and serve at once.

Picture on next page: stuffed eggplant

chicken and rice dinner

Yield: 4 to 6 servings

2 to 3 pounds chicken, cut into serving pieces
¼ cup flour
2 tablespoons shortening
1 package onion soup
½ cup white rice
1 cup water
1 can cream of mushroom soup

Dredge chicken pieces in flour.

Heat shortening in cooker; brown the chicken. Add onion soup, rice, and water. Close cover of cooker and put pressure control in place. When pressure is reached, cook for 15 minutes. Allow to cool naturally. Remove cover of cooker.

On a very low flame, stir in the cream of mushroom soup so that all is blended thoroughly.

Serve at once.

island chicken dinner

Yield: 4 to 6 servings

2 tablespoons shortening
1 onion, sliced
1 garlic clove, crushed
2½-pound chicken, cut into serving pieces
1 cup boneless ham or pork, cut into small cubes
2 tomatoes, chopped
1 cup diced sweet potatoes
2 carrots, diced
1 cup diced yellow squash
1 tablespoon parsley
1 bay leaf
½ teaspoon oregano
1 teaspoon salt
1 cup chicken broth

Heat shortening. Brown onion, garlic, and then chicken pieces. Add rest of ingredients in order given. Close cover of cooker and put pressure control in place. When pressure is reached, cook for 10 minutes. Allow cooker to cool normally.

Stir and serve.

rained-out chicken dinner

This dish was thrown together on a night the little-league baseball game was rained out and no dinner was planned. It was so good, it's worth repeating anytime.

Yield: 4 to 6 servings

> 1 cup rice
> 1 cup green beans, cut into
>   1-inch pieces
> 1 medium onion, quartered
> 1 green pepper, diced
> 2 cups canned tomatoes
>   (1-pound can)
> 1 teaspoon salt
> ½ cup water
> 1 cup diced cooked chicken

Put rice, beans, onion, green pepper, tomatoes, salt, and water in cooker. Close cover and set pressure regulator in place. When pressure is reached, cook for 2 minutes. Allow cooker to cool naturally.

Remove regulator and cover and return open pot to a low flame. Add the diced chicken and simmer until hot.

Serve the chicken dinner with a salad.

brunswick stew

Yield: 4 to 6 servings

> 2 to 3 pounds stewing chicken, cut into serving pieces
> 2 medium onions, sliced
> 1 cup corn
> 1 cup lima beans
> 1 green pepper, diced
> 2 tomatoes, quartered
> 1 tablespoon salt
> Dash of Tabasco sauce
> ¼ teaspoon pepper
> 1 cup water
> 1 cup seasoned croutons (optional)

Put ingredients into cooker in order given. Close cover and put pressure regulator in place. When pressure is reached, cook for 20 minutes. Cool cooker at once.

Optional but good—stir in 1 cup of seasoned croutons, and serve.

Picture on opposite page: rained-out chicken dinner

fish teriyaki

Yield: 4 to 6 servings

> 2 pounds fish fillets, cut into 2-inch pieces
> Teriyaki sauce to cover the fish
> 1 cup rice
> 2 cups canned tomatoes with juice
> ½ cup water

Marinate the fish in enough teriyaki sauce to cover for at least 1 hour.

Place both fish and marinade in cooker. Add rice, tomatoes, and water. Close cover and put pressure control in place. When pressure is reached, cook for 5 minutes. Cool cooker normally for 5 minutes, then reduce pressure under running water.

Use bamboo shoots and water chestnuts in your salad to complete the dinner.

fish in tureen

Yield: 6 to 8 servings

> 2 pounds haddock, cut into bite-size pieces
> 2 cups water
> 2 cups diced onions
> 2 cups diced potatoes
> ½ cup rice
> 1 large green pepper, diced
> ½ to 1 cup chopped celery
> ½ cup diced carrots
> 2 tablespoons salt
> 3 whole peppercorns
> 2 tablespoons minced parsley

Place ingredients in cooker in order listed. Close cover and set pressure control in place. When pressure is reached and control jiggles gently, cook for 5 minutes. Allow pressure to drop naturally.

Serve this in a large tureen, and complete the meal with a tossed salad.

hambolaya

Yield: 4 to 6 servings

> 1 cup rice
> 1 cup corn
> 1 cup green beans
> 1 medium onion, quartered
> 1 green pepper, diced
> 2 cups canned tomatoes (1-pound can)
> 1 teaspoon salt
> ½ cup beef broth
> 1 cup cooked ham, diced

Put all ingredients except the ham into the cooker in the order given. Close cover and put pressure control in place. When pressure is reached, cook for 3 minutes. Allow pressure to drop of its own accord.

Remove regulator and cover and return open cooker to a low light. Add diced ham and stir until all flavors blend and all is piping hot. Serve.

seafood stew

Use your imagination for the fish. Include some scallops or some shelled clams or shrimp. The mixed fish will add flavor to this stew.

Yield: 4 to 6 servings

    2 tablespoons shortening
    1 large onion, sliced
    1 garlic clove, crushed
    2 pounds mixed fish, cut into chunks
    1 or 2 tomatoes, peeled and chopped
    1 cup diced potatoes
    ¼ cup chopped parsley
    1 teaspoon salt
    Dash of pepper
    1 cup dry white wine

Heat shortening. Brown onion and garlic. Add the rest of the ingredients in order given. Close cover and put pressure control in place. When pressure is reached, cook for 3 minutes. Cool cooker at once under running water. Serve.

tuna, rice, and broccoli

If crepes are your thing, this would make a delicious filling for your own special crepe dinner.

Yield: 4 to 6 servings

    1½ pounds broccoli, cut into 1-inch pieces,
        or 2 10-ounce packages frozen cut broccoli
    2 tablespoons lemon juice
    ¼ teaspoon dillseed
    1 13-ounce can tuna
    ½ cup rice
    1 cup water
    1 can condensed cream of celery soup
        (or your preference of any cream soup)

Combine the broccoli, lemon juice, dillseed, tuna, rice, and water in the pressure cooker. (If frozen broccoli is used, break up each block into 1-inch pieces.) Put cover on cooker in locked position, with pressure regulator in place. When pressure is reached, cook for 2 minutes, then remove from heat. Allow to cool naturally. Remove the cooker lid.

Using a wooden spoon, stir in the condensed cream of celery soup, mixing thoroughly.

Serve at once.

desserts

a word about desserts

Because it is an ideal steamer, the pressure cooker lends itself well to the making of many desserts. The heat attained is constant, which produces a uniform texture in the cooked foods.

The use of molds is required in the preparation of steamed puddings and custards. For this, individual custard cups of the standard size may be used. For a large pudding or bread recipe, a 1-quart aluminum or metal mold or an ovenproof bowl will serve well. If the recipe requires that the mold be covered, aluminum foil makes a good cover, as it shapes well to the mold.

Because a larger quantity of water is used in the steaming process, you may find water stains on the interior of the cooker. To avoid this, add 1 teaspoon of vinegar or ½ teaspoon of cream of tartar to the water required. This will help avoid water stains.

Do *not* cook applesauce, cranberries, or rhubarb in the pressure cooker. Such foods tend to foam or froth and may block the vent pipe.

brown betty

Yield: 4 to 6 servings

1 cup dry bread crumbs
¼ cup sugar
1 teaspoon cinnamon
1 lemon, juice and rind
3 apples, cored and sliced
¼ cup melted butter
2 cups water

Mix bread crumbs, sugar, cinnamon, and lemon juice and rind.

Lightly grease the bowl to be used. Alternate layers of apples and crumb mixture in greased bowl. Pour melted butter over ingredients. Cover bowl tightly with aluminum foil.

Put water and rack in cooker. Place bowl on rack. Close cover securely; put pressure regulator in position. When pressure is reached, cook for 15 minutes. Cool cooker at once under running water.

Serve the Brown Betty at room temperature.

Variation: Add ½ cup raisins to the bread-crumb mixture.

brown bread

Yield: About 30 slices

  2 eggs, beaten
  2 tablespoons butter, melted
  ⅔ cup molasses
  1 teaspoon baking soda
  1 cup buttermilk
  1 cup all-purpose flour
  1 teaspoon baking powder
  ½ teaspoon salt
  2 cups whole-wheat flour
  1 cup seeded raisins
  4 cups water

Prepare for this recipe by setting aside 3 tin cans (1-pound 4-ounce size). Grease the insides and bottoms of the empty cans well.

Stir eggs, butter, and molasses together.

In a 2-cup measure, mix baking soda with buttermilk.

Sift together white flour, baking powder, salt, and whole-wheat flour.

Alternately add buttermilk mixture and flour to egg mixture. Last, add raisins; stir well. Fill the waiting tin cans half full; cover tightly with foil.

Put 4 cups water and the rack in cooker. Set the cans on rack; close cover securely. Do *not* put pressure control on. Allow a small stream of steam to escape from cooker for 1½ hours. Remove cooker from heat. Let stand 5 minutes more, then open.

Your loaves are ready for butter or cream cheese. So good.

date and nut bread

Yield: 10 to 12 servings

  1 egg
  ½ cup sugar
  1 cup milk
  2½ cups flour
  2 teaspoons baking powder
  ½ teaspoon salt
  ½ cup chopped dates
  ½ cup chopped nuts
  4 cups water

Beat egg and sugar together.

Measure milk.

Sift dry ingredients together. Alternate milk and dry ingredients to form the dough. Last, stir in dates and nuts.

Grease 1-quart mold; pour dough into it. Cover with aluminum foil.

Put water and rack into cooker. Set mold on rack; close cover securely. Do *not* put pressure control on cooker. Allow a small stream of steam to flow from vent pipe for 1½ hours. Remove cooker from heat. Let stand 5 minutes, then open.

nut bread

Yield: 10 to 12 servings

> **1 egg**
> **½ cup sugar**
> **1 cup milk**
> **2½ cups flour**
> **2 teaspoons baking powder**
> **½ teaspoon salt**
> **1 cup chopped nuts**
> **4 cups water**

Beat eggs together with sugar until frothy. Alternate adding the milk with the sifted dry ingredients. Last, stir in nuts.

Grease 1-quart mold; pour nut-bread dough into it. Cover mold with aluminum foil.

Put water and rack into cooker. Set mold on rack; close cover of cooker securely. Do *not* put pressure control on cooker. Allow a small stream of steam to flow from vent pipe for 1½ hours. Remove cooker from heat. Let stand 5 minutes, then open.

custard

Yield: 4 servings

> **2 cups milk**
> **2 eggs, beaten**
> **⅓ cup sugar**
> **¼ teaspoon salt**
> **½ teaspoon vanilla**
> **Dash of nutmeg**
> **½ cup water**

Scald the milk in a saucepan; allow to cool slightly.

Combine eggs, sugar, and salt in a bowl. Add slightly cooled milk slowly, stirring constantly. Add vanilla. Pour mixture into individual custard cups; sprinkle each serving with some nutmeg. Cover each cup with aluminum foil.

Place water in cooker; put rack in place. Put custard cups on rack; close cover securely. Put pressure control in place. When pressure is reached, cook for 3 minutes. Cool at once.

Chill the custards before serving.

chocolate custard

Yield: 4 to 6 servings

    3 cups hot milk
    1 square grated chocolate
    3 eggs
    3 tablespoons sugar
    1½ teaspoons vanilla
    ¼ teaspoon salt
    1 cup water

Melt grated chocolate in hot milk. Set aside to cool slightly.

Mix eggs, sugar, vanilla, and salt. Gradually add chocolate milk, stirring constantly. Pour into 1-quart mold. Cover mold with foil.

Put water and rack into pressure cooker. Set mold on rack; close cover securely. Put pressure regulator in place. When pressure is reached, cook for 7 minutes. Remove cooker from heat; allow to cool normally.

Chill the custard before serving.

peppermint-candy custard

Yield: 4 servings

    2 cups milk
    2 eggs, beaten
    ½ cup ground peppermint-stick candy
    ¼ teaspoon salt
    ½ teaspoon vanilla
    ½ cup water

Scald the milk; set aside to cool slightly.

Combine eggs, candy, and salt in a bowl. Gradually add milk and vanilla, stirring constantly. Pour mixture into individual custard cups. Cover each cup tightly with aluminum foil.

Place water in cooker; set rack in place. Put custard cups on rack; close cover securely. Put pressure control in place. When pressure is reached, cook for 3 minutes. Cool at once under running water.

Chill the custards before serving.

bread pudding

Yield: 4 to 6 servings

> 3 slices stale bread, cubed
> 1 tablespoon melted butter or margarine
> ¼ teaspoon salt
> ½ cup brown sugar
> 1 teaspoon cinnamon
> 2 cups hot milk
> 2 eggs, slightly beaten
> ½ teaspoon vanilla
> ½ cup raisins
> ½ cup chopped nuts
> 4 cups water

Put bread in mixing bowl. Add all ingredients in order given. Mix well.

Gently pour bread mixture into well-greased mold that will set loosely in your cooker. Cover mold with aluminum foil.

Put water and rack in cooker. Put mold on top of rack. Close cover securely. Do *not* put pressure control on yet. Allow cooker to steam for 5 minutes, then put pressure control in place. When pressure is reached, cook for 15 minutes. Allow pressure to drop of its own accord.

steamed chocolate pudding

Although this recipe takes time in the kitchen, it is easy, good, and well worth including here.

Yield: 10 to 12 servings

> 3 tablespoons butter
> ⅔ cup sugar
> 1 egg
> 2¼ cups all-purpose flour
> 4½ teaspoons baking powder
> ¼ teaspoon salt
> 1 cup milk
> 2½ ounces baking chocolate, melted
> 4 cups water

Cream butter and sugar thoroughly. Add egg; mix well.

Sift dry ingredients together; add to creamed mixture alternately with milk. Stir in melted chocolate.

Grease 1-quart mold; pour mixture into it. Cover with aluminum foil.

Put water and rack into cooker. Add covered mold. Close cooker cover. Allow a small stream of steam to escape from vent for 1½ hours. Do *not* use pressure control. Remove cooker from heat. Let stand 5 minutes.

Serve the pudding with your favorite hard sauce.

date and nut rice pudding

Yield: 4 to 6 servings

> **2 cups milk**
> **2 eggs, slightly beaten**
> **⅓ cup brown sugar**
> **½ teaspoon salt**
> **⅔ cup cooked rice**
> **½ teaspoon vanilla**
> **½ cup chopped dates**
> **½ cup walnuts**
> **½ cup water**

Heat but do not boil milk. Allow to cool slightly.

Combine eggs, sugar, and salt in a bowl. Add milk slowly, stirring constantly. Add rice, vanilla, dates, and walnuts. Pour mixture into custard cups. Cover each cup with aluminum foil.

Put water and rack in cooker; place custard cups on rack. Close cover; put pressure control in place. When pressure is reached, cook for 3 minutes. Cool cooker at once under running water.

Uncover custard cups and stir slightly before chilling in refrigerator.

fresh-fruit cocktail

Yield: 4 to 6 servings

> **½ pound peaches, diced**
> **¼ pound pears, diced**
> **¼ pound apricots, diced**
> **2 sticks cinnamon**
> **1 teaspoon lemon juice**
> **1¼ cups water**
> **Sugar to taste**

Prepare fruit by coring, paring, and dicing into small pieces.

Place rack in pressure cooker. Put fruit on rack. Add cinnamon sticks.

Mix lemon juice with water; pour over fruit. Close cover securely; put pressure control in place. When pressure is reached and regulator rocking gently, remove from heat. Cool at once under running water. Add sugar to taste while liquid is hot enough to dissolve it. Stir gently.

Allow fruit to cool, and serve slightly chilled.

dried-fruit compote

Do not fill the cooker over two-thirds full. This allows for the expansion of the fruit.

Yield: 4 to 6 servings

½ pound dried apricots
½ pound dried peaches
½ pound dark raisins
3 cups water

Soak fruit in water 1 hour. Reserve this water to be used when cooking.

Place fruit in cooker and pour water in which it soaked over it, adding water, if needed, to make 3 cups. Close cover of cooker; put pressure control in place. When pressure is reached, cook for 3 to 5 minutes. Cool cooker at once under running water. Add sugar to taste, if desired.

fresh spiced peaches

Yield: 4 to 6 servings

1 pound peaches, peeled, seeded, and halved
2 sticks cinnamon
1 teaspoon lemon juice
1¼ cups water
Sugar to taste

Put prepared fruit on rack in cooker. Add cinnamon sticks.

Mix lemon juice in water; pour over fruit. Close cover of cooker; put pressure control in place. When pressure is reached, cook for 2 minutes. Cool at once under running water. Add sugar to taste.

Serve the peach halves chilled.

spiced peaches and pears

Yield: 4 to 6 servings

½ pound dried peaches
½ pound dried pears
2 cups water
½ cup sugar
6 whole cloves
2 sticks cinnamon
2 pieces gingerroot (optional)

Soak fruit in water for 1 hour before cooking.

Place fruit and 2 cups water in cooker; close cover securely. Put pressure control in place. When pressure is reached, cook for 4 minutes. Cool cooker at once under running water.

Return cooker to stove uncovered. Add sugar, cloves, cinnamon, and gingerroot; cook on low heat 5 minutes more. Allow to cool. Serve.

mint pears

Yield: 4 to 6 servings

> **1 pound pears, cored, pared, and quartered**
> **½ cup sugar**
> **1¼ cups water**
> **3 tablespoons crème de menthe**

Place pears on rack in cooker.

Mix sugar in water until dissolved; pour over pears. Close cover securely; put pressure control in place. When pressure is reached, cook for 2 minutes. Cool at once under running water. Allow fruit to cool completely. When pears are cold, add creme de menthe.

Serve the pears with meat or as a dessert.

spiced pineapple

Yield: 4 to 6 servings

> **1 cup sugar**
> **1 cup vinegar**
> **½ cup water**
> **2 sticks cinnamon**
> **20 whole cloves**
> **1 whole pineapple, peeled, cored, and sliced**

Place sugar, vinegar, water, and spices in cooker. Boil together 5 minutes. Put pineapple slices into liquid. Close cover of cooker; put pressure control in place. When pressure is reached, cook for 5 minutes. Cool at once under running water.

spiced prunes

These prunes may be a good addition to a meat course as well as being a tasty dessert.

Yield: 4 to 6 servings

> **1 pound dried prunes**
> **2 cups water**
> **½ lemon, sliced**
> **1 stick cinnamon**

Soak prunes in 2 cups water at least 1 hour. Fruit will puff up with the water.

When ready to cook prunes, place them in cooker with water in which they soaked and enough extra water to make up 2 full cups. Add sliced lemon and cinnamon stick. Close cover of cooker; put pressure control in place. When pressure is reached, cook for 5 minutes. Cool cooker at once under running water.

If you prefer your prunes slightly sweetened, add sugar to taste and stir the fruit in the open cooker over low heat for 1 minute more.

questions and answers about pressure cooking

Q. *Most recipes in this book are for 4 to 6 people. My family is small and I frequently want to cook smaller quantities. Is there any difference when small quantities are cooked in a 4-quart pressure cooker?*

A. Smaller quantities of food may be cooked in the pressure cooker with the same good results as the larger quantities. The food will still retain more of its own flavor, and time—that important saving of minutes—will still work to your advantage. If you are cooking for a smaller family and still want to prepare the larger quantities for 4 to 6 people, plan to freeze half of what you prepare for another meal.

Q. *I cooked potatoes and they turned dark and unattractive in the cooker. What did I do wrong?*

A. Potatoes may darken in a pressure cooker if they are cooked too long. This is also true of certain other vegetables, such as cauliflower and other light-colored vegetables. Occasionally the water in certain localities will make vegetables darken. While this may change the eye appeal of these vegetables, it in no way takes away from the taste or nutritional value.

Q. *Do I have to season foods before cooking them?*

A. It is not necessary to season foods before cooking them, and sometimes it is a good idea not to do so. Pressure-cooked foods retain more of the natural mineral salts and flavors than foods cooked in any other manner. Most people do not use as much seasoning with a pressure cooker as they do with ordinary cooking. Adding seasonings to taste after foods are cooked is often a good idea.

Q. *Why must I sear a roast on all sides before cooking it?*

A. If you do not sear the meat well on all sides, you may find you get an excess of gravy when preparing the larger cuts of meat. There is no evaporation with pressure cooking, so it is important that the meat be thoroughly sealed in to retain those juices in the meat itself.

Q. *Sometimes my meat sticks to the bottom of the cooker. What can I do to avoid this?*

A. When preparing to sear meat, first heat the cooker without the cover. Heat the cooker thoroughly before the fat or shortening is added. Use a little more fat than called for in the hot cooker. This should help eliminate the problem of sticking meat.

Q. *What causes sticking and burning on the bottom of the cooker during the cooking period?*

A. If liquid is lost during the cooking period, food may stick. There are several things to check on to avoid this problem. Check the condition of the sealing ring. If it needs replacement, do so. Do not let the pressure control wiggle violently during the cooking period. This is not necessary for good performance of the pressure cooker. A gentle rocking motion will cook all foods. Another factor to watch is to be sure you close the cover of the cooker immediately after adding the required amount of water. Last, be sure you have the required amount of water—or a little extra—in the cooker. These are reasons foods may stick to the cooker. Sticking and burning can be easily avoided.

Q. *I cooked carrots in the pressure cooker twice. The first time they cooked tender in the required time. The second time they were tough. Why?*

A. Carrots and some other foods may dehydrate slightly when they have been stored over a period of time. This leaves a tough fiber that makes the food more difficult to cook. If you are using food that has been stored for some time, increase the time allowed for cooking by 1 or 2 minutes extra.

Q. *What about frozen meat? Can I take a piece of meat right from the freezer and cook it in the pressure cooker?*

A. Yes, you can cook meat right from the freezer, but it is better to at least partially thaw the meat. That allows complete contact with the bottom of the cooker for browning on all sides. If you're up against it, though, and must cook a piece of frozen meat, increase the cooking time. Cook beef and veal approximately 25 minutes per pound. Cook pork 30 minutes per pound. You can expect more gravy this way, but the end result will still be delicious.

Q. *What about one-pot dinners? Can vegetables and meat be cooked together?*

A. Yes, yes, yes. There is a section of this cookbook dealing solely with one-pot dinners. The rule to be guided by is to cook foods together that need the same amount of cooking time. Potatoes, carrots, and many other vegetables can be cooked with chops or cut-up stew meats. Let the necessary amount of cooking time and the flavor combinations dictate what may be cooked together.

Q. *Cooking times baffle me. One roast will take a certain amount of time to cook. Another roast of the same weight may take longer. Why?*

A. The weight of a piece of meat is not the only factor that determines how long it will need to cook. Two pounds of stew meat take less cooking time than a 2-pound flank steak. The cooking time depends on the thickness of the meat as well as its weight. Also, consider the kinds of meat. Pork and mutton take longer to cook, regardless of their weight, than the same size piece of beef. Young, properly aged meat will take less time than old, tough, stringy meat. One thing is certain, though. Even that old, tough, stringy meat will cook up tender in a pressure cooker when given enough time. Check your recipes for proper timing, and consider the piece of meat you want to cook. This combination will assure you of a tender, tasty meal.

Q. *Can I cook two or more vegetables at the same time?*

A. Yes, indeed. If the vegetables to be cooked require the same amount of cooking time, there is no reason not to cook them together. However, do use your rack.

Put the required amount of water in the cooker, then add the rack, and place the vegetables on the rack. In this way, each vegetable will retain its own flavor and still cook tender.

Q. *How delicate is the pressure control? May I wash it?*

A. The pressure regulator is not so delicate that you must be afraid of it. It is always better not to drop it, but even that will probably not do it any damage. As for washing it, use warm soapy water and leave it out to dry thoroughly.

Q. *When should I put the pressure control on the cooker?*

A. All recipes in this book say to close the cover of the cooker securely. When the cover is closed and the handles meet, put the pressure control in place. You will know that the proper pressure is reached when the control jiggles gently. There are a few recipes included here that include steaming of breads and puddings. Follow those recipe directions as to when to place the pressure regulator in position.

Q. *How often should the sealing ring be changed?*

A. When the sealing ring or gasket no longer holds steam, it needs to be replaced. How often this needs to be done depends on how often you use your pressure cooker. Rubber does tend to lose its elasticity, and, when this happens, consult your parts pages in the book that came with your cooker, and order the necessary new parts.

Q. *Can I remove the cover from the cooker while the pressure regulator is in place?*

A. NO! The pressure control is one of your most important safety factors. As long as it is on the cooker, there is a possibility that there is still pressure in the cooker. The procedure is to cool the cooker first under running water—or allow it to cool naturally. When you are sure the cooker is cool, remove the pressure control. Then, and only then, remove the cover.

Q. *Many recipes do not say anything about using the cooking rack. When should it be used in the cooker?*

A. The purpose of the rack is to keep food out of the cooking liquid. In many recipes, this is neither necessary nor desirable. For example, a stew cooks nicely in its own essence. If you are cooking vegetables, however, and want them steamed, use the cooking rack to keep the vegetables above the liquid.

Q. *Some recipes say "Cool at once under running water." Others say "Allow to cool naturally." Why?*

A. When a recipe calls for cooling the cooker at once, the cooking time is complete, and the food in the cooker is ready to eat. However, some foods benefit from the longer cooking time. By allowing the cooker to cool of its own accord, you are allowing the extra cooking time that is needed for that particular recipe.

Q. *How can I adapt my pressure cooker to high altitude?*

A. Cooking time should be increased 5 percent for every 1,000 feet above the first 2,000 feet. The time increases as follows:

> 3,000 feet. . . 5%
> 4,000 feet. . . 10%
> 5,000 feet. . . 15%
> 6,000 feet. . . 20%
> 7,000 feet. . . 25%
> 8,000 feet. . . 30%

Q. *I have a favorite recipe that I want to prepare in the pressure cooker. How can I adapt my recipe to pressure cooking?*

A. To adapt your favorite recipe, look at the directions for the same type of food you want to cook. Decide on the amount of liquid needed in your recipe. You will use less liquid in the pressure cooker than you did in other cooking. Use at least ½ cup more liquid than you want in the finished food. Cooking time can be decreased by two-thirds for the pressure cooker.

index

144